"Cultivating the art of mind reading is not about invading privacy, but about deepening connections. It's a journey of empathy, understanding, and unlocking the hidden layers of human thought and emotion. As we master the techniques, we open doors to profound insights, transformative connections, and a world where understanding becomes our superpower."

The Art of Mind Reading: 40 Techniques for Unveiling Thoughts and Motivations

Rami Georgiev

Published by Rami Georgiev, 2023.

THE ART OF MIND READING: 40 TECHNIQUES FOR UNVEILING THOUGHTS AND MOTIVATIONS

First edition. July 2, 2023.

ISBN: 979-8223719120

Written by Rami Georgiev.

Dedication:

To the seekers of truth, the empathetic souls, and the compassionate hearts who yearn to understand the intricacies of human existence, this book is lovingly dedicated to you. It is for those who are not content with surface-level interactions but seek to delve deep into the labyrinth of human thoughts, motivations, and emotions.

For all the curious minds who strive to break down the barriers that separate us, who long to foster empathy and forge authentic connections, this dedication is a testament to your unwavering commitment. It is a tribute to your unwavering belief that by understanding others, we gain invaluable insights into ourselves and the world around us.

May the wisdom contained within these pages ignite a flame of curiosity within you, guiding you on a transformative journey of self-discovery and profound connection. May you uncover the hidden layers of the human psyche, transcending the limitations of mere observation and truly stepping into the shoes of others.

This dedication is a heartfelt expression of gratitude for your unwavering pursuit of understanding, for your willingness to embrace the complexity of the human experience, and for your dedication to fostering compassion and empathy in a world that sometimes seems to have forgotten their significance.

May this book be your trusted companion as you navigate the intricacies of human interaction, offering insights, techniques, and guidance to deepen your understanding of others and, in turn, yourself. May it empower you to bring about positive change, bridging divides, and cultivating a world where empathy, understanding, and connection are cherished above all.

To all those who believe that true understanding has the power to transform lives and make the world a better place, this dedication is for you. Thank you for embarking on this journey of exploration and for embracing the profound impact that understanding can have on our relationships, our communities, and our shared humanity.

Introduction:

Welcome, my dear friends, to a transformative journey of the mind—a voyage that will unveil the profound art of mind reading. In these pages, we embark on a quest to understand the intricate workings of the human psyche, to decipher the hidden thoughts and motivations that shape our every interaction.

In a world bustling with noise and distractions, we often find ourselves yearning for deeper connections, a genuine understanding of others, and the ability to truly empathize. This longing, my friends, is what brings us together, bound by a shared desire to unravel the mysteries of human behavior and forge meaningful relationships.

"The Art of Mind Reading: 40 Techniques for Unveiling Thoughts and Motivations" is not a mere guidebook—it is a doorway to a new dimension of understanding. Here, we shall explore the extraordinary power of perception, empathy, and observation. We shall learn how to interpret the subtle cues and unspoken language that lie beneath the surface of our everyday interactions.

Each chapter is dedicated to a unique technique, a treasure waiting to be uncovered. From decoding facial expressions and understanding body language to delving into the realms of personality typing and motivation decoding, we shall explore the rich tapestry of techniques that empower us to read minds and uncover the intricate web of human thoughts and motivations.

But, my dear friends, this journey is not one of manipulation or invasion of privacy. No, it is a journey steeped in compassion, empathy, and the genuine desire to connect with our fellow human beings on a deeper level. It is a path that leads us to embrace our shared vulnerabilities and recognize the threads of humanity that bind us together.

As we delve into the depths of mind reading, let us remember that true understanding begins with ourselves. It is an inner exploration—a mirror reflecting our own fears, desires, and motivations. By honing our skills of perception and empathy, we not only unravel the thoughts and emotions of others but also gain profound insights into our own selves.

Throughout this transformative voyage, I invite you to embrace a mindset of curiosity and open-mindedness. Let us set aside judgment and preconceived notions, and instead, approach each technique with a sense of wonder and genuine interest. For it is through this lens that we unlock the true power of mind reading—not as a parlor trick, but as a means to build bridges, foster compassion, and bring positive change to our lives and the lives of those around us..

Dear friends, I am honored to be your guide on this extraordinary expedition into the realm of mind reading. Let us embark upon this voyage with an open heart and a thirst for knowledge, ready to uncover the intricate tapestry of thoughts, motivations, and emotions that lie within ourselves and in the souls of others. Together, we shall transcend boundaries, deepen connections, and embrace a world where understanding becomes our compass, leading us to a brighter and more compassionate future.

Technique 1 - The Power of Observation

Welcome, my dear friends, to the very first technique on our journey of mind reading—the exquisite art of observation. In a world that often moves at a relentless pace, the ability to pause, observe, and truly see becomes a transformative skill that opens doors to profound understanding.

Observation is not a passive act but an active engagement with the world around us. It is about cultivating a keen sense of awareness, attuning our senses to the nuances of behavior, body language, and subtle shifts in expression. By honing our powers of observation, we unlock a wealth of information, glimpses into the thoughts and motivations that drive human actions.

Imagine, my friends, walking into a crowded room—a symphony of voices, gestures, and emotions. In this sea of bustling activity, the power of observation becomes our compass, guiding us through the labyrinth of human interaction. By keenly observing the dynamics at play, we gain insights into the unspoken stories that dance within each person.

Let us delve deeper into the realms of observation. Take a moment to imagine sitting in a café, observing the interactions of those around you. Notice the subtle shifts in body language—the crossed arms, the furrowed brows, the genuine smiles that light up faces. Each gesture, each expression holds a key to unraveling the thoughts and emotions beneath the surface.

But observation is not limited to external cues alone. It extends to the realm of self-awareness—a journey of deep introspection. By observing our own thoughts, feelings, and patterns of behavior, we gain a deeper understanding of our own motivations. We recognize the echoes of our past experiences that shape our present actions.

To truly embrace the power of observation, we must cultivate a sense of curiosity, a thirst for understanding. Let us become mindful detectives, detectives of the human experience. Pay attention to the details, the subtleties that may go unnoticed by others. Notice the shifts in tone, the microexpressions that flash across faces, the energy that vibrates in the spaces between words.

Allow me to share an example, my dear friends, to illustrate the transformative power of observation. Imagine a couple engaged in a heated argument. The words they exchange are merely the tip of the iceberg, for beneath the surface lies a treasure trove of emotions—hurt, fear, and longing. By keenly observing their body language, the tension in their shoulders, the sadness in their eyes, we begin to glimpse the underlying motivations that fuel their conflict.

The art of observation is not a skill that comes naturally to all, but it is one that can be cultivated through practice and intention. Let us commit ourselves to the art of seeing, of truly noticing the world around us. Through observation, we become more attuned to the human experience, more empathetic to the joys and struggles that color our interactions.

Dear friends, as we embark upon this journey of mind reading, let us embrace the power of observation as our foundation. By honing this skill, we unlock a world of insights, creating bridges of understanding, and fostering deep connections. Together, let us embark upon this transformative exploration, where observation becomes our lens to unravel the mysteries of the human experience.

Technique 2 - Reading Facial Expressions

Welcome to the enchanting realm of decoding facial expressions, where the language of emotions is etched upon the human face. Our faces, adorned with a tapestry of muscles, serve as windows to our innermost thoughts and feelings, inviting us to embark on a journey of understanding and connection.

The human face is a canvas of expression, portraying a symphony of joy, sorrow, surprise, and myriad other emotions. Each subtle movement, each fleeting expression carries profound meaning, offering us glimpses into the intricate landscapes of the human experience.

As we delve into the art of mind reading, facial expressions become our guiding stars, illuminating the unspoken stories that reside within each individual. They transcend barriers of language and culture, speaking a universal language that enables us to forge deep connections with others. By mastering the art of reading facial expressions, we unlock the ability to interpret the emotions that color our interactions.

Let us embark upon a deeper exploration of the nuances of facial expressions. Picture a moment of pure delight—a heartfelt laugh that ripples through the air. The eyes twinkle with mirth, the lips curve upward, and the entire face radiates with happiness. In that ephemeral instant, a world of joy unfolds, inviting us to share in the blissful experience.

But, my dear seekers of understanding, facial expressions extend far beyond moments of jubilation. They also serve as windows into the depths of pain, sadness, and fear. A furrowed brow, a downturned mouth, or a gaze averted—these delicate cues provide us with a glimpse into the emotional tapestry that lies beneath the surface.

To truly decipher facial expressions, we must cultivate the art of keen observation, attuning ourselves to the subtlest movements and microexpressions. It is within these fleeting gestures that the true gems of insight are discovered. By honing this skill, we unlock a world of emotions that often go unnoticed by the casual observer.

Allow me to share a few captivating examples that illustrate the transformative power of reading facial expressions. Imagine encountering a loved one, their countenance adorned with a genuine smile that reaches their eyes. In that moment, their face becomes a beacon of warmth, radiating affection and fostering a profound sense of connection.

Now, envision a colleague who enters the room burdened by invisible woes. Their eyes betray a weariness that contradicts their words. Through astute observation of their facial expressions—the furrowed brow, the downturned lips—we gain insight into their inner turmoil. Armed with this understanding, we can approach them with compassion, offering support and a listening ear.

Furthermore, picture a friend confiding in you, their face a tapestry of vulnerability and anguish. As they share their story, their facial expressions morph—subtle shifts in their brow, a tear glistening in their eye. By attentively deciphering these cues, we can validate their emotions, providing solace and empathy during their time of need.

Dear seekers of connection, as we embark upon the path of mind reading, let us embrace the power of decoding facial expressions as a key to unlocking the emotions that saturate our interactions. Through this technique, we gain profound insights into the human experience, fostering empathy and nurturing bonds that transcend words.

May our journey through the intricacies of facial expressions be one of deep empathy and understanding, as we recognize the profound impact our own expressions can have on others. Approach this technique with reverence and a genuine desire to forge meaningful connections. By attuning ourselves to the silent language of the face, we become architects of empathy and cultivators of authentic human connection.

Together, let us explore this mesmerizing world, where faces become storytellers, and the art of reading facial expressions becomes a transformative skill on our quest for deeper understanding and more profound connections.

Technique 3 - Decoding Body Language

Welcome, fellow seekers of insight, to the captivating realm of deciphering body language—a silent symphony of gestures and movements that reveal the hidden narratives of human communication. In this chapter, we embark on a transformative journey to unravel the profound messages conveyed through the language of the body.

The body, my dear companions, is a remarkable vessel of expression—a canvas upon which emotions, intentions, and inner thoughts are artfully displayed. Every tilt of the head, shift in posture, or movement of limbs carries meaning, whispering tales that words alone cannot convey.

As we delve into the art of mind reading, body language becomes our compass, guiding us through the labyrinth of human interaction. It offers a treasure trove of cues, providing valuable insights into a person's state of mind, level of engagement, and underlying emotions.

Let us explore the intricate nuances of body language, where every gesture becomes a brushstroke in the masterpiece of nonverbal communication. Picture a person standing tall, shoulders back, exuding confidence and self-assuredness. Their expansive posture commands attention, projecting an air of authority and presence.

But body language is not confined to displays of confidence alone. It also reveals vulnerabilities and insecurities that lie beneath the surface. Picture someone crossing their arms tightly, their body turned away, creating a shield of self-protection. These closed-off gestures communicate defensiveness or discomfort, offering a glimpse into their emotional landscape.

To truly decode body language, we must become astute observers, attuned to the subtleties of movement and positioning. It is in the interplay of gestures, the synchrony of body and mind, that we uncover the hidden meanings. By honing this skill, we open the door to a world of understanding and connection.

Allow me to share a multitude of captivating examples that illuminate the transformative power of decoding body language. Imagine a job interview, where a candidate leans forward, maintaining direct eye contact with the interviewer, and subtly mirroring their movements. These open and engaged gestures communicate enthusiasm, genuine interest, and a desire to establish rapport, making a lasting impression.

Now, picture a tense conversation between two individuals. As emotions escalate, their bodies mirror the intensity—a tightening of fists, a clenched jaw, or a rapid pacing of steps. These nonverbal cues speak volumes, foretelling the depth of their emotions and highlighting the need for empathy, active listening, and effective communication to diffuse the tension.

Furthermore, imagine attending a social gathering where you observe a person fidgeting, avoiding eye contact, and constantly shifting their weight from foot to foot. These gestures betray a sense of discomfort or anxiety, signaling an opportunity for compassion and creating a safe space for them to feel accepted. By extending a gentle hand of reassurance or engaging in open-ended conversation, we can help them feel more at ease and encourage their participation.

In another scenario, envision a couple sitting side by side, their bodies turned towards each other, leaning in attentively, and their expressions mirroring each other's joy and contentment. These synchronized gestures communicate a deep bond, trust, and emotional connection that transcends words.

Dear seekers of understanding, as we delve into the art of decoding body language, let us embrace the power it holds to enhance our interactions and deepen our connections. Through this technique, we gain valuable insights into the unspoken narratives that shape our relationships and can navigate social situations with empathy and grace.

May our journey through the intricacies of body language be one of keen observation, intuition, and empathy, as we recognize the profound impact that nonverbal cues can have on our interactions. Let us approach this technique with a sense of curiosity and a genuine desire to forge meaningful connections.

Together, let us explore this captivating world, where bodies become storytellers, and the art of decoding body language becomes a transformative skill on our quest for authentic human connection and understanding.

Technique 4 - Voice and Tone Analysis

In this chapter, we embark on a transformative journey into the depths of voice and tone analysis—an exploration of the hidden dimensions that lie within the very sound of our words. Prepare to discover the power of listening beyond the surface, as we uncover the nuances of vocal expressions.

The human voice, my dear companions, is a vessel of emotions, intentions, and unspoken messages. It carries the essence of our being, painting a vivid tapestry of our inner world. By honing the art of voice and tone analysis, we unlock the ability to decode these intricacies and gain a deeper understanding of the people we encounter.

Imagine engaging in a conversation with someone whose voice exudes confidence and clarity. The resonance of their words, the measured pace, and the unwavering tone captivate your attention. This commanding presence draws you in, igniting a sense of respect and trust.

Now, picture a voice that trembles with nervousness or hesitation. The subtle quivers, the wavering cadence—it reveals vulnerability and uncertainty. By attuning ourselves to these subtleties, we can offer support, encouragement, and create a safe space for others to find their voice and express themselves authentically.

Voice and tone analysis extends beyond the surface-level observations of pitch and volume. It allows us to discern the underlying emotions beneath the words spoken. Imagine hearing a voice laced with joy, its infectious energy reverberating in every syllable. This exuberant expression invites celebration and connection.

On the other hand, envision a voice touched by sadness or grief—a voice that carries the weight of a heavy heart. Its somber timbre and gentle intonations speak volumes about the inner struggles and pain experienced by the speaker. By truly listening, we can extend empathy, support, and a compassionate presence.

Let me share a multitude of captivating examples that illuminate the transformative power of voice and tone analysis. Imagine a motivational speaker, their voice booming with enthusiasm and passion. The rise and fall of their intonations ignite a fire within, inspiring and energizing their audience to embrace their own potential.

Consider a scenario where you engage in a heartfelt conversation with a close friend. As they recount a personal story, their voice quivers with vulnerability, allowing you to glimpse their emotional landscape. By attentively listening to the nuances of their voice, you can offer comfort, understanding, and a shoulder to lean on.

Now, picture a leader who addresses a crowd with a tone of authority and conviction. Their voice resounds with power, capturing the attention and commanding respect. By analyzing their vocal presence, we gain insight into their leadership style and their ability to inspire others to action.

Additionally, imagine a parent consoling their child, their voice adopting a soothing, nurturing tone. The gentle rhythm and tender inflections communicate love and reassurance, creating a sense of safety and trust for the little one.

Dear seekers of understanding, as we venture into the realm of voice and tone analysis, let us embrace the immense potential it holds in our interactions. By actively listening to the melodies of the human voice, we can unlock a deeper level of connection, empathy, and understanding.

May our journey through the nuances of vocal expressions be one of genuine curiosity, compassionate listening, and the profound recognition that every voice carries a unique story. Let us cultivate the skill of voice and tone analysis, allowing it to enhance our relationships, amplify our impact, and foster harmonious connections.

Together, let us explore the captivating world of voice and tone analysis, where the echoes of our words transcend their surface meaning, and the true essence of our being is unveiled in every syllable.

Chapter 5: Technique 5 - Developing Empathy

In this chapter, we embark on a transformative journey into the realm of empathy—a virtue that has the power to bridge divides, heal wounds, and foster deep human connection. Prepare to embark on a path of heartfelt compassion and learn the art of developing empathy.

Empathy, my dear companions, is the ability to understand and share the feelings of others. It is a profound act of stepping into someone else's shoes, immersing ourselves in their world, and experiencing life through their lens. By developing empathy, we cultivate a profound capacity to connect with others on a deeper level, to understand their struggles, and to offer genuine support.

Imagine a world where empathy reigns supreme—a world where we listen not only with our ears but also with our hearts. In this world, we seek to understand before we seek to be understood. We become compassionate observers, attuned to the emotions and experiences of those around us.

Developing empathy begins with active listening—an intentional practice of giving our undivided attention to others. When someone shares their story, we resist the urge to interrupt or offer immediate advice. Instead, we create a safe space for them to express themselves fully, without judgment or interruption.

Empathy extends beyond words—it involves tuning into non-verbal cues, sensing the unspoken emotions that lie beneath the surface. It is in the gentle touch of a hand, the comforting smile, or the understanding nod that we convey our presence and willingness to connect on a profound level.

Let us delve into the depths of empathy and its transformative power through a multitude of captivating examples. Imagine a friend sharing their struggles with anxiety—an invisible battle that affects their daily life. By listening with empathy, we create a space of understanding, providing solace and support without diminishing their experiences.

Now, picture a colleague going through a difficult time, burdened by professional challenges. Through the lens of empathy, we acknowledge their struggles, offering encouragement, and lending a helping hand. We recognize that their journey is unique, and our empathy becomes a catalyst for their growth and resilience.

Empathy also allows us to appreciate the perspectives of those different from ourselves. Imagine engaging in a conversation with someone whose cultural background, beliefs, or experiences differ from your own. Through empathy, we open ourselves to new insights, shedding light on diverse narratives and fostering a more inclusive society.

Developing empathy is not limited to our interactions with others. It also involves cultivating self-empathy—a deep understanding and acceptance of our own emotions and experiences. By embracing self-empathy, we nurture self-compassion, recognizing that we too are deserving of kindness, understanding, and forgiveness.

Dear seekers of connection, as we embark on the path of developing empathy, let us open our hearts to the experiences of others. Let us cultivate the ability to truly see and understand their emotions, challenges, and dreams. In doing so, we create a world where compassion becomes the guiding force, where understanding transcends boundaries, and where human connection thrives.

May our journey into the depths of empathy be one of continuous growth, genuine curiosity, and heartfelt connection. Let us become beacons of empathy in a world that yearns for understanding and unity. Together, let us learn and practice the art of developing empathy, transforming our relationships, communities, and the very fabric of our existence.

Technique 5 - Developing Empathy

In this chapter, we embark on a transformative journey into the realm of empathy—a virtue that has the power to bridge divides, heal wounds, and foster deep human connection. Prepare to delve into the art of developing empathy and learn how to cultivate this transformative quality within yourself.

Empathy, my dear companions, is the ability to understand and share the feelings of others. It is a profound act of stepping into someone else's shoes, immersing ourselves in their world, and experiencing life through their lens. By developing empathy, we cultivate a profound capacity to connect with others on a deeper level, to understand their struggles, and to offer genuine support.

Imagine a world where empathy reigns supreme—a world where we listen not only with our ears but also with our hearts. In this world, we seek to understand before we seek to be understood. We become compassionate observers, attuned to the emotions and experiences of those around us.

Developing empathy begins with active listening—an intentional practice of giving our undivided attention to others. When someone shares their story, we resist the urge to interrupt or offer immediate advice. Instead, we create a safe space for them to express themselves fully, without judgment or interruption.

Empathy extends beyond words—it involves tuning into non-verbal cues, sensing the unspoken emotions that lie beneath the surface. It is in the gentle touch of a hand, the comforting smile, or the understanding nod that we convey our presence and willingness to connect on a profound level.

Let us explore the transformative power of empathy through a multitude of captivating examples. Imagine a friend going through a difficult breakup, their heart heavy with sorrow. Through empathy, we offer a compassionate ear, validating their emotions and providing a shoulder to lean on.

Now, picture a colleague experiencing work-related stress, overwhelmed by deadlines and expectations. By empathizing with their situation, we create an environment of support and understanding. We lend a helping hand or offer words of encouragement, acknowledging the challenges they face.

Empathy also allows us to appreciate the perspectives of those different from ourselves. Imagine engaging in a conversation with someone whose cultural background, beliefs, or experiences differ from your own. Through empathy, we open ourselves to new insights, shedding light on diverse narratives and fostering a more inclusive society.

Developing empathy is not limited to our interactions with others. It also involves cultivating self-empathy—a deep understanding and acceptance of our own emotions and experiences. By embracing self-empathy, we nurture self-compassion, recognizing that we too are deserving of kindness, understanding, and forgiveness.

Dear seekers of connection, as we embark on the path of developing empathy, let us open our hearts to the experiences of others. Let us cultivate the ability to truly see and understand their emotions, challenges, and dreams. In doing so, we create a world where compassion becomes the guiding force, where understanding transcends boundaries, and where human connection thrives.

May our journey into the depths of empathy be one of continuous growth, genuine curiosity, and heartfelt connection. Let us become beacons of empathy in a world that yearns for understanding and unity. Together, let us learn and practice the art of developing empathy, transforming our relationships, communities, and the very fabric of our existence.

Technique 6 - Emotional Intelligence

Welcome, seekers of emotional mastery. In this chapter, we embark on a profound exploration of emotional intelligence—a skill that empowers us to understand, manage, and navigate the vast landscape of emotions. Prepare to embark on a transformative journey as we delve into the art of emotional intelligence and unlock its boundless potential.

Emotional intelligence, my fellow travelers, is the ability to recognize, understand, and regulate both our own emotions and those of others. It is a skill that allows us to navigate the intricate web of human emotions with grace and wisdom. By developing emotional intelligence, we gain profound insights into ourselves and the world around us, fostering stronger relationships, making wiser decisions, and living a more fulfilled life.

Imagine a world where emotional intelligence reigns—a world where we approach each interaction with empathy, understanding, and a genuine desire to connect. In this world, we navigate the ebbs and flows of emotions with a profound sense of self-awareness, embracing the beauty and complexity of our own emotional landscape.

Developing emotional intelligence begins with self-awareness—an unwavering commitment to exploring our own emotions, thoughts, and patterns of behavior. It is through this deep self-reflection that we gain insights into our triggers, strengths, and areas for growth. By cultivating self-awareness, we become attuned to our own emotional state, allowing us to respond rather than react to the world around us.

Emotional intelligence also involves recognizing and understanding the emotions of others—a skill known as empathy.

Through empathy, we develop the capacity to truly listen, connect, and offer support to those around us. It is in the delicate balance of understanding our own emotions and empathizing with others that emotional intelligence flourishes.

Let us embark on a journey through the realm of emotional intelligence, guided by a multitude of captivating examples. Picture a challenging conversation with a loved one—an exchange fraught with anger and frustration. With emotional intelligence, we strive to remain calm and composed, seeking to understand their perspective, and responding with empathy and compassion.

Now, envision a professional setting—a team facing a significant setback or failure. Through emotional intelligence, we create an environment of psychological safety, fostering open communication and providing support to navigate through difficult emotions. We offer encouragement, acknowledge individual contributions, and facilitate a collective healing process.

Emotional intelligence also empowers us to manage our own emotions effectively, even in the face of adversity. Imagine a high-pressure situation, where stress threatens to overwhelm us. Through emotional intelligence, we develop strategies to regulate our emotions, practicing self-care, and adopting healthy coping mechanisms. We channel our emotions constructively, making decisions with clarity and composure.

Dear seekers of emotional intelligence, as we delve into the depths of this transformative skill, let us embrace the full range of human emotions, honoring their presence and seeking to understand their messages. Let us cultivate self-awareness, empathy, and the ability to regulate our emotions with wisdom and grace.

May our journey into the realm of emotional intelligence be one of growth, resilience, and profound connection. Let us become guardians of emotional mastery, navigating the vast ocean of emotions with compassion, understanding, and authenticity. Together, let us unlock the power of emotional intelligence and embark on a life imbued with wisdom, fulfillment, and profound human connection.

In the next chapter, we will explore Technique 7, a powerful tool for enhancing our emotional intelligence. Get ready to uncover the art of self-reflection, as we delve into the practice of introspection and gain deeper insights into ourselves and the world around us.

Technique 7 - Active Listening

In this chapter, we embark on a transformative exploration of active listening—a skill that holds the key to deep understanding, genuine empathy, and meaningful communication. Prepare to delve into the art of active listening and discover its immense power in fostering authentic connections.

Active listening, my dear companions, is more than just hearing words—it is the art of fully engaging with the speaker, both verbally and non-verbally. It is a practice that involves giving our undivided attention, suspending judgment, and creating a safe space for open expression. By developing active listening skills, we cultivate a powerful tool for building trust, strengthening relationships, and unraveling the depths of human experiences.

Imagine a world where active listening becomes the norm—a world where we honor each conversation as an opportunity for connection and growth. In this world, we set aside our own agendas and distractions, immersing ourselves in the present moment, and truly hearing the words and emotions behind them.

Developing active listening begins with presence—an unwavering commitment to being fully engaged in the conversation at hand. It is about setting aside our own thoughts and concerns, and offering our complete attention to the speaker. By being present, we create a sacred space for authentic expression and connection.

Active listening also involves non-verbal cues—a language spoken through gestures, facial expressions, and body language. It is in maintaining eye contact, nodding in understanding, and mirroring the speaker's emotions that we convey our genuine interest and support.

Through these non-verbal cues, we signal that we are fully present and ready to listen.

Let us embark on a journey through the art of active listening, guided by a multitude of captivating examples. Imagine a friend sharing their dreams and aspirations. With active listening, we resist the urge to interject with our own experiences or opinions. Instead, we encourage them to delve deeper, asking open-ended questions that invite further exploration and self-reflection.

Now, picture a loved one confiding in us about their fears and insecurities. Through active listening, we create a safe space for vulnerability, allowing them to express themselves without judgment. We offer words of comfort, empathize with their emotions, and assure them that their feelings are valid and acknowledged.

Active listening is equally essential in professional settings. Imagine a team meeting where diverse perspectives clash. Through active listening, we foster an environment of inclusivity and respect, seeking to understand the viewpoints of all team members. We listen attentively, acknowledging the value of each contribution, and striving for collaborative solutions.

Dear seekers of profound connection, as we delve into the depths of active listening, let us open our hearts and minds to the experiences of others. Let us embrace the power of presence, non-verbal cues, and genuine curiosity. By cultivating active listening skills, we forge deeper connections, foster understanding, and create a world where authentic communication thrives.

May our journey into the realm of active listening be one of continuous growth, genuine curiosity, and heartfelt connection. Let us become ambassadors of this transformative skill, enriching our relationships, communities, and the very fabric of our existence.

In the next chapter, we will explore Technique 8, a powerful tool for enhancing our ability to connect with others on a deeper level. Get ready to uncover the art of empathy, as we delve into the practice of understanding and embracing the emotions and experiences of those around us.

Technique 8 - Perspective-Taking

In this chapter, we embark on a profound exploration of perspective-taking—a transformative skill that enables us to transcend our own point of view and embrace the rich tapestry of human experiences. Get ready to expand your horizons and develop a profound sense of empathy as we delve into the art of perspective-taking.

Perspective-taking, dear companions, is the ability to step into the shoes of another, to see the world through their eyes, and to understand their thoughts, emotions, and motivations. It is a practice that invites us to set aside our biases, preconceived notions, and judgments, and to truly embrace the diversity of human perspectives. By cultivating perspective-taking, we open ourselves to new insights, forge deeper connections, and foster a world built on compassion and understanding.

Imagine a world where perspective-taking becomes a way of life—a world where we seek to understand rather than to be understood, and where differences are celebrated rather than feared. In this world, we recognize that every person carries a unique story, shaped by their experiences, beliefs, and cultural backgrounds. Through perspective-taking, we bridge the gaps of misunderstanding, foster empathy, and build a foundation of authentic connection.

Developing perspective-taking begins with curiosity—an insatiable thirst for knowledge about the diverse perspectives that exist around us. It is through curiosity that we challenge our own assumptions and actively seek to learn from others. By approaching conversations with an open mind and genuine interest, we create a space for individuals to share their stories and perspectives without fear of judgment.

Let me share a powerful example of perspective-taking in action. Imagine meeting someone from a different cultural background, with customs and traditions that may seem unfamiliar to you. By cultivating perspective-taking, you embrace the opportunity to explore their culture with genuine curiosity and respect. You ask open-ended questions, listen attentively to their experiences, and appreciate the beauty and depth of their traditions. Through this act of perspective-taking, you not only expand your own understanding but also foster a sense of connection and unity.

Now, envision a situation where conflicts arise due to differing viewpoints on a particular issue. Through perspective-taking, you engage in deep listening and empathetic dialogue. You strive to understand the underlying motivations and beliefs that shape each perspective. By genuinely seeking to comprehend the reasoning behind different viewpoints, you create an atmosphere of respect and openness, fostering the potential for collaborative solutions and harmonious resolutions.

Perspective-taking also empowers us to challenge our own biases and prejudices. It prompts us to examine our deeply ingrained assumptions and to actively seek out diverse perspectives. By intentionally seeking alternative viewpoints, we expand our understanding of the world, cultivate empathy, and break down the barriers that divide us.

Let me share another example to illustrate the power of perspective-taking. Imagine encountering someone who holds radically different political or ideological beliefs from your own. Rather than engaging in heated arguments or dismissing their views outright, you practice perspective-taking. You engage in genuine conversations, seeking to understand the underlying values and experiences that have shaped their worldview. Through this act of perspective-taking, you not only deepen your empathy and understanding but also create opportunities for constructive dialogue and finding common ground.

Dear seekers of expanded understanding, as we delve into the depths of perspective-taking, let us embrace the beauty of human diversity and the wisdom that lies within each individual. Let us cultivate curiosity, active listening, and a genuine desire to connect. By practicing perspective-taking, we lay the foundation for a more compassionate and inclusive world.

May our journey into the realm of perspective-taking be one of humility, empathy, and profound growth. Let us become ambassadors of this transformative skill, inspiring others to embrace the richness of diverse perspectives and fostering a global community built on mutual understanding and respect.

Technique 9 - Personality Typing

Welcome, seekers of insight and self-discovery, to the realm of personality typing. In this chapter, we embark on a journey to unravel the intricacies of human personality, exploring a transformative technique that can deepen our understanding of ourselves and others. Get ready to explore the captivating world of personality typing and unlock the keys to greater self-awareness and harmonious relationships.

Personality typing is a powerful tool that allows us to categorize and understand the patterns of behavior, thoughts, and preferences that shape our unique identities. It helps us recognize that each individual possesses a distinctive blend of traits and tendencies, influencing how they perceive the world and interact with others. By delving into the realm of personality typing, we gain valuable insights into ourselves and develop a heightened appreciation for the diversity of human personalities.

Imagine, dear companions, being able to understand the driving forces behind your own behavior—the motivations, strengths, and areas for growth that shape your journey. Through personality typing, we gain clarity about our natural inclinations and the ways in which we perceive and engage with the world. It becomes a compass, guiding us toward self-acceptance and providing a framework for personal growth.

Personality typing not only illuminates our own paths but also enhances our interactions with others. By recognizing the unique personality types of those around us, we foster a deeper understanding and empathy for their perspectives, communication styles, and needs.

This insight becomes a bridge that bridges the gaps of misunderstanding and strengthens our connections with others.

Let us delve into the fascinating world of personality typing and explore a few prominent frameworks that can serve as guides on our journey of self-discovery and understanding.

One widely recognized model is the Myers-Briggs Type Indicator (MBTI), which categorizes individuals into sixteen distinct personality types based on their preferences in four key dimensions: extraversion or introversion, sensing or intuition, thinking or feeling, and judging or perceiving. Through the MBTI, we gain insights into our preferred ways of gathering information, making decisions, and approaching the world around us.

For example, let's consider the INFJ personality type—an introverted, intuitive, feeling, and judging type. INFJs are often known for their deep empathy, strong intuition, and ability to understand others on a profound level. They possess a natural inclination toward helping and inspiring others, and their insights often come from a deep well of intuition and emotional intelligence.

Another influential framework is the Enneagram, which offers nine distinct personality types, each characterized by a core motivation and set of behaviors. The Enneagram dives deep into the underlying fears, desires, and defense mechanisms that drive our actions. By exploring our Enneagram type, we gain a profound understanding of our core motivations and the patterns that shape our lives.

Consider, for instance, the Type 5, often known as "The Investigator." Type 5 individuals have a thirst for knowledge, a desire to understand the world around them, and a tendency to withdraw into their own thoughts and inner worlds. They value privacy, intellectual pursuits, and seek to conserve their energy by carefully selecting their social engagements.

Dear seekers of insight, as we venture into the realm of personality typing, let us approach this exploration with openness and curiosity.

Remember that these frameworks serve as guides, not rigid boxes that confine us. They offer valuable insights, but they do not define who we are entirely. Embrace the richness of your own unique personality and celebrate the diversity that exists within the human experience.

Technique 10 - Analyzing Behavior Patterns

In this chapter, we embark on an enlightening exploration of behavior patterns—an invaluable technique that allows us to decode the intricacies of human actions and gain a deeper comprehension of ourselves and others. Get ready to unravel the mysteries that lie beneath our behaviors and discover the transformative power of analyzing behavior patterns.

Behavior patterns, dear companions, are the repeated actions, reactions, and habits that shape our lives. They provide glimpses into our inner workings, revealing our underlying motivations, fears, and desires. By delving into the realm of behavior patterns, we develop a heightened awareness of our own actions and gain the ability to decipher the messages conveyed by the behaviors of those around us.

Imagine, dear seekers, the power of understanding the behavioral patterns that govern your own life. By analyzing your actions and reactions, you gain insights into your unconscious patterns, bringing them into the light of consciousness. This newfound awareness becomes a catalyst for personal growth, as you recognize the patterns that support your well-being and identify those that may hinder your progress. With this understanding, you can consciously choose to reinforce positive patterns and break free from self-limiting behaviors.

Let us explore a variety of examples to illustrate the profound impact of analyzing behavior patterns in our lives.

1. Jenny, a diligent student, consistently procrastinates on her assignments and studies at the last minute. Through analyzing her behavior patterns, she realizes that she is driven by a fear of failure and

perfectionism. Armed with this insight, she can implement strategies such as breaking tasks into smaller, manageable chunks and practicing self-compassion, ultimately improving her productivity and reducing stress.

2. Michael, a team leader at work, notices that he frequently becomes impatient and dismissive when team members present new ideas. By analyzing his behavior patterns, he discovers that his reaction stems from a deep-seated need for control and a fear of change. With this newfound understanding, he can consciously work on creating an environment that fosters open communication, collaboration, and innovation.

3. Sarah, a mother of two, often finds herself getting frustrated and yelling at her children when they misbehave. Through analyzing her behavior patterns, she uncovers that her own stress and exhaustion contribute to her reactions. With this awareness, she can implement self-care practices, seek support, and develop effective parenting strategies that promote a more peaceful and harmonious family dynamic.

Analyzing behavior patterns also enhances our understanding of others and paves the way for more harmonious relationships. Let's imagine a scenario where a colleague consistently interrupts others during meetings. Instead of becoming annoyed or disregarding their input, by analyzing their behavior patterns, we might discover that they have a strong need for validation and recognition. With this insight, we can approach the situation with empathy, actively listen to their ideas, and create a supportive environment that allows them to contribute meaningfully.

Dear seekers of profound understanding, as we delve into the realm of analyzing behavior patterns, let us embrace the power of self-reflection and observation. Cultivate a curious and compassionate mindset as you explore your own patterns and those of others. Remember that behavior patterns are complex and multifaceted, influenced by a myriad of factors such as upbringing, past experiences, and personal beliefs. Approach the analysis with patience, understanding that unraveling these patterns is a lifelong journey.

Technique 11 - Motivation Decoding

In this chapter, we embark on a transformative journey to unravel the intricate web of human motivations—those driving forces that shape our thoughts, actions, and aspirations. Prepare yourself to unlock the secrets of motivation, gain a profound understanding of what truly moves us, and harness this knowledge to navigate the vast landscapes of personal growth and meaningful connections.

Motivation, dear companions, is the invisible spark that ignites our desires, propels us forward, and fuels our pursuit of dreams. It is the compass that guides our decisions, shapes our habits, and determines the paths we choose to walk. By delving into the depths of motivation, we uncover the core drivers that propel individuals to achieve greatness, overcome obstacles, and find fulfillment in their lives.

Imagine, dear seekers, the power of deciphering the intricate language of motivation. By understanding our own motivations, we gain invaluable insights into what inspires and drives us. We peel back the layers of our desires and discover the underlying values, passions, and aspirations that propel us forward. With this self-awareness, we can align our actions with our truest selves, cultivate a sense of purpose, and embark on a journey of growth and fulfillment.

Let us explore a multitude of examples to illuminate the power of Motivation Decoding in our lives:

1. Emily, a dedicated entrepreneur, is driven by a deep desire for financial independence and the opportunity to make a positive impact on the world. By decoding her motivations, she understands that her strong work ethic and perseverance stem from her core values of autonomy and contributing to a greater cause. With this clarity, Emily

can align her business ventures with her passion for social entrepreneurship, creating a meaningful and purpose-driven career.

2. David, an aspiring musician, uncovers that his motivation to create soul-stirring melodies is rooted in a profound need for self-expression and emotional connection. By decoding his motivations, he recognizes that his music serves as a conduit for sharing his deepest emotions and connecting with others on a profound level. With this understanding, David can infuse his compositions with authenticity, creating art that resonates with the hearts of his listeners.

3. Sarah, a dedicated healthcare professional, discovers that her unwavering commitment to patient care arises from a deep-seated empathy and a genuine desire to alleviate suffering. By decoding her motivations, she realizes that her purpose is not merely to heal the physical ailments of her patients but also to provide them with comfort, compassion, and hope. With this newfound insight, Sarah can approach her work with even greater empathy, going beyond the call of duty to make a difference in the lives of those she serves.

As we decode motivations, we also gain a profound understanding of others and forge deeper connections. Imagine encountering a friend who has embarked on a weight loss journey. By decoding their motivations, we might uncover that their desire to lead a healthier lifestyle stems from a yearning for self-acceptance and improved self-confidence. Armed with this insight, we can offer support, encouragement, and understanding, fostering a nurturing environment that empowers them to achieve their goals.

Cultivate a keen awareness of the invisible threads that weave the tapestry of motivation, both within ourselves and in the people we encounter. Remember that motivations are deeply personal and may evolve over time, influenced by experiences, values, and evolving priorities. Approach the decoding process with sensitivity and respect, honoring the uniqueness of each individual's journey.

Technique 12 - Contextual Analysis

In this chapter, we embark on a profound exploration of the intricate interplay between behavior and context—a powerful technique that enables us to unravel the hidden nuances and underlying meanings of human actions. Prepare to deepen your understanding of the complex tapestry of human behavior, as we delve into the fascinating world of contextual analysis and unlock the keys to profound insights and empathic connections.

Context, dear companions, serves as the backdrop against which our behaviors unfold. It encompasses the multitude of factors that shape our experiences, perceptions, and reactions. By delving into the realm of contextual analysis, we unravel the invisible threads that connect our actions to the surrounding environment, social dynamics, cultural influences, and personal histories. This exploration illuminates the profound impact that context has on our behaviors and provides a gateway to understanding the motives, intentions, and deeper meanings behind them.

Imagine, dear seekers, the power of contextual analysis in unraveling the complexity of human behavior. By examining the situational factors that shape our actions, we gain profound insights into the why and how of our choices. We move beyond surface-level judgments and delve into the underlying layers of influence that guide our responses. With this heightened awareness, we can navigate the complexities of interpersonal relationships, enhance our empathic connections, and cultivate a deep understanding of the human experience.

Let us explore a diverse range of examples to illuminate the transformative nature of contextual analysis:

1. In a heated argument between two friends, a contextual analysis unveils the underlying factors that contribute to their conflict. By considering their past experiences, communication styles, and emotional states, we gain a deeper understanding of the triggers and dynamics at play. Armed with this insight, we can approach the situation with empathy, compassion, and a willingness to seek common ground, fostering reconciliation and growth.

2. A team project encounters unexpected challenges, leading to frustration and tension among team members. Through contextual analysis, we uncover external factors such as time constraints, conflicting priorities, and communication breakdowns. By understanding these contextual elements, we can devise strategies to address the root causes of conflict, foster collaboration, and realign the team towards shared goals.

3. A leader implementing organizational changes recognizes the importance of contextual analysis to navigate the complexities of the transition. By considering the existing company culture, individual concerns, and the broader industry landscape, they can craft a thoughtful change management plan that addresses specific challenges and fosters employee engagement and buy-in.

Contextual analysis also empowers us to extend our understanding beyond our immediate surroundings and embrace diverse perspectives. By examining the cultural, societal, and historical contexts that shape the behavior of individuals from different backgrounds, we bridge the gaps of understanding and foster inclusivity. Through contextual analysis, we appreciate the rich tapestry of human experiences and honor the uniqueness of each person's journey.

Cultivate a keen awareness of the invisible forces at play, recognizing that behaviors do not exist in isolation but are deeply intertwined with the context in which they unfold. Approach the analysis process with humility and respect, honoring the complexities and intricacies of human behavior.

Technique 13 - Microexpressions and Microgestures

In this chapter, we embark on a fascinating journey into the realm of subtle nonverbal cues—the fleeting flashes of emotions and gestures that offer profound insights into the hidden realms of human communication. Prepare to enhance your understanding of the unspoken language that lies beneath the surface, as we explore the intricate world of microexpressions and microgestures and unlock the keys to profound connections and heightened perception.

Microexpressions, dear companions, are the fleeting facial expressions that occur within a fraction of a second, revealing our true emotions before our conscious mind can mask them. They are the authentic windows to the soul, the silent messengers that convey unfiltered emotions such as joy, sadness, surprise, fear, disgust, and anger. Microgestures, on the other hand, encompass the subtle movements and postures of our bodies, conveying additional layers of meaning and intention.

Imagine, dear seekers, the power of decoding microexpressions and microgestures in unraveling the mysteries of human interaction. By honing our ability to observe and interpret these subtle cues, we gain profound insights into the emotions, intentions, and hidden narratives of those around us. We become adept at reading between the lines, deciphering the unspoken messages, and cultivating authentic connections that transcend words alone.

Let us explore a multitude of examples to illuminate the transformative nature of microexpressions and microgestures:

1. Sarah, during a business meeting, briefly furrows her brow and tenses her lips, indicating a fleeting moment of concern or disagreement. By recognizing this microexpression, we can address her unvoiced concerns, open up the space for dialogue, and build trust within the team.

2. John, in a social gathering, involuntarily displays a microgesture of leaning forward and tilting his head slightly while engaging in conversation with a friend. This subtle movement signifies attentiveness, genuine interest, and an inclination to listen actively. By reciprocating this gesture, we deepen the connection and create an environment of mutual understanding and respect.

3. Emma, during a high-pressure presentation, reveals a microexpression of a suppressed smile, indicating a subtle sense of confidence and excitement. By perceiving this fleeting expression, we can offer words of encouragement and create a supportive atmosphere that allows her to shine and deliver her best.

The art of decoding microexpressions and microgestures extends beyond individual interactions. It applies to various contexts, including negotiations, interviews, public speaking, and conflict resolution. By recognizing the unspoken emotions and intentions, we navigate these situations with heightened sensitivity, empathy, and adaptability.

Cultivate the art of being fully present, attuned to the subtle dances of emotions and movements that occur beneath the surface. Approach the decoding process with compassion and respect, honoring the complexities and uniqueness of each individual's nonverbal communication.

Technique 14 - Statement Analysis

In this chapter, we embark on a transformative journey into the art of decoding spoken and written words—the intricate tapestry of language that reveals deeper meanings, intentions, and underlying truths. Prepare to sharpen your analytical skills and unlock the power of words as we delve into the profound world of statement analysis, unraveling the hidden messages and narratives that lie within.

Statements, dear companions, are not mere arrangements of words; they carry profound significance and hold the potential to unveil the intricate workings of the human mind. By delving into the practice of statement analysis, we embark on a journey of exploration, unraveling the layers of meaning, subconscious cues, and underlying motivations that shape our expressions. Through this art, we cultivate a deep understanding of the unspoken messages and unlock the keys to empathetic connections and authentic dialogue.

Imagine, dear seekers, the power of statement analysis in uncovering the deeper truths and intentions that lie beneath the surface. By honing our skills in decoding the intricacies of language, we gain the ability to discern authenticity from deception, empathy from manipulation, and clarity from confusion. With this heightened awareness, we navigate the complexities of communication with finesse, cultivating deeper connections and fostering harmonious relationships.

Let us explore a multitude of examples to illuminate the transformative nature of statement analysis:

1. In a heartfelt conversation with a loved one, they share their dreams and aspirations, but their statement is punctuated with phrases

like "I hope" or "someday." By analyzing these subtle linguistic markers, we uncover underlying doubts or insecurities, and we can offer support, encouragement, and guidance to help them overcome obstacles and pursue their dreams with conviction.

2. In a business negotiation, a potential partner makes a statement such as, "Our company values integrity and transparency above all." However, upon closer analysis, we notice inconsistencies between their words and actions. This insight prompts us to exercise caution, dig deeper into their motives, and ensure alignment between their proclaimed values and their actual practices.

3. In a written letter of complaint, a customer describes their experience with a product, using vivid imagery and emotional language. Through statement analysis, we uncover the underlying emotions, frustrations, and desires behind their words. Armed with this understanding, we can respond with empathy, address their concerns, and foster customer loyalty and satisfaction.

Statement analysis empowers us to move beyond surface-level understanding and delve into the rich tapestry of human expression. It helps us decipher the hidden narratives, unspoken desires, and emotional undercurrents that shape our interactions. By honing this skill, we embrace the power of discernment and foster genuine connections built on understanding, trust, and mutual respect.

Dear seekers of profound understanding, as we venture deeper into the realm of statement analysis, let us embrace the power of active listening, careful observation, and a willingness to explore the layers of meaning embedded within words. Approach the analysis process with a spirit of curiosity and humility, recognizing that language is a nuanced and dynamic tool that reflects the complexities of the human experience.

Technique 15 - Reading Emotional Energy

In this chapter, we embark on a profound journey into the realm of subtle energies—the unseen vibrations that envelop us and shape our emotional experiences. Prepare to expand your awareness and tap into the powerful currents of emotional energy as we delve into the transformative world of empathetic perception, unlocking the keys to heightened intuition and profound connections.

Emotional energy, dear companions, is the invisible force that flows within and around us, influencing our thoughts, feelings, and interactions with others. It is the subtle hum of emotions that colors our experiences, leaving indelible imprints on our souls. By delving into the art of reading emotional energy, we gain access to a deeper level of understanding—one that transcends words and transcends physical appearances.

Imagine, dear seekers, the power of reading emotional energy in navigating the complex landscape of human interactions. By honing our ability to perceive these subtle energetic signals, we become attuned to the emotions that lie beneath the surface, whether they are our own or those of others. With this profound insight, we navigate the waters of life with heightened sensitivity and empathy, forging connections that bridge the gaps of misunderstanding and enriching our relationships with authenticity and compassion.

Let us explore a multitude of examples to illuminate the transformative nature of reading emotional energy:

1. In a crowded room filled with laughter and celebration, you notice a friend who appears joyful on the outside, but your empathetic

perception detects a subtle undercurrent of sadness in their eyes. By attuning to their emotional energy, you extend a caring hand and offer a safe space for them to share their inner feelings, fostering a deeper bond of trust and support.

2. In a professional setting, you encounter a colleague who seems agitated and on edge. Rather than dismissing their behavior as mere irritability, your heightened awareness of emotional energy prompts you to inquire gently, uncovering the stressors that lie beneath and offering your assistance in navigating challenges.

3. During a conversation with a loved one, you pick up on a vibrant and uplifting emotional energy that permeates their words and gestures. In response, you share moments of joy and laughter, allowing the positive energy to amplify and strengthen the emotional connection between you both.

Reading emotional energy is a skill that transcends cultural and linguistic barriers. It connects us on a profound level, bridging the gaps of miscommunication and fostering an atmosphere of understanding and unity. By cultivating this skill, we enrich our lives with moments of genuine connection, empathy, and shared emotional experiences.

Dear seekers of profound understanding, as we venture deeper into the realm of reading emotional energy, let us embrace the power of mindfulness, presence, and heart-centered awareness. Approach this practice with an open heart, free from judgment, and be receptive to the subtle vibrations that flow through every interaction. By connecting with our intuitive selves and embracing our innate empathetic abilities, we awaken the dormant power within us and become catalysts for positive change in our lives and the lives of others.

In the next chapter, we will explore Technique 16, a transformative method for harnessing emotional energy in challenging situations. Get ready to embark on a journey of emotional resilience, as we learn to transmute negative energy, cultivate emotional balance, and emerge stronger in the face of adversity. Together, let us tap into the wellspring of emotional wisdom and transform our lives with profound self-awareness and compassionate understanding.

Technique 16 - Emotional Framing

Welcome, dear seekers, to the enlightening exploration of Emotional Framing. In this chapter, we embark on a transformative journey into the realm of perception and interpretation of emotions—the art of shaping our emotional experiences through conscious framing. Prepare to expand your emotional intelligence and harness the power of intentional framing as we delve into the depths of this profound technique, unlocking the keys to emotional well-being and empowered living.

Emotional framing, dear companions, is the practice of consciously directing our thoughts, beliefs, and perspectives to shape our emotional experiences. It is the art of choosing how we interpret and respond to the myriad of emotions that arise within us and in our interactions with the world. By exploring the depths of emotional framing, we gain mastery over our emotional landscape, empowering ourselves to navigate life's challenges with grace and resilience.

Imagine, dear seekers, the power of emotional framing in transforming the way we perceive and experience the world. By consciously framing our emotions, we become architects of our own emotional landscapes, building a foundation of positivity, resilience, and well-being. With this empowering skill, we can reshape our outlook, release limiting beliefs, and embrace emotions as allies on our path to personal growth and fulfillment.

Let us explore a multitude of examples to illuminate the transformative nature of emotional framing:

1. In the face of a setback or failure, rather than succumbing to despair and self-doubt, we can choose to frame the experience as an

opportunity for growth and learning. By reframing our perspective, we open ourselves to valuable lessons, resilience, and the possibility of even greater success in the future.

2. When faced with a challenging relationship, instead of allowing anger or resentment to consume us, we can reframe the situation as an opportunity for compassion, understanding, and personal growth. By shifting our perspective, we cultivate empathy, foster deeper connections, and transform the dynamics of the relationship.

3. In moments of stress and overwhelm, rather than being overwhelmed by negative emotions, we can intentionally frame the situation as an invitation to practice mindfulness, self-care, and stress management techniques. By reframing stress as an opportunity for personal growth and self-care, we empower ourselves to cultivate inner peace and well-being.

Emotional framing empowers us to break free from limiting patterns of thought and embrace the boundless possibilities of our emotional experiences. It is a powerful tool that allows us to shape our reality, nurture positive emotions, and transcend challenging circumstances with resilience and grace.

Dear seekers of profound understanding, as we venture deeper into the realm of emotional framing, let us embrace the power of conscious awareness, mindfulness, and intentional thought. Approach this practice with a spirit of curiosity and self-compassion, recognizing that our thoughts and interpretations hold the key to transforming our emotional landscape. By harnessing the power of emotional framing, we unlock our potential for emotional mastery and create a life imbued with purpose, joy, and authentic fulfillment.

Technique 17 - Intuition and Gut Feeling

This chapter, we embark on a journey of self-discovery and deep inner knowing as we explore the remarkable power of our intuitive senses. Prepare to awaken your intuition, trust your gut instincts, and tap into a wellspring of wisdom that surpasses logical reasoning and rationality.

Intuition, dear companions, is the innate ability we all possess to perceive and understand information beyond the scope of our conscious awareness. It is the whisper of wisdom that emerges from the depths of our being, guiding us with an instinctual knowingness that transcends logic. By honing our intuition and embracing our gut feelings, we gain access to a powerful compass that can navigate us through the complexities of life.

Imagine, dear seekers, the extraordinary potential that lies within the realm of intuition. By cultivating a deep connection with our intuitive senses, we become attuned to the subtle vibrations of the world around us and within us. We tap into a wellspring of wisdom that can guide us in decision-making, relationships, and pursuing our life's purpose. With intuition as our ally, we navigate the labyrinth of life with clarity, trust, and unwavering confidence.

Let us explore a myriad of examples to illuminate the transformative nature of intuition and gut feeling:

1. In moments of uncertainty, you may feel a deep sense of unease or hesitation within your gut. Your intuition gently nudges you to pause, reflect, and reconsider your choices. By heeding this inner guidance, you avoid potential pitfalls and make decisions aligned with your highest good.

2. When meeting someone for the first time, your intuition may provide subtle cues that alert you to their true intentions. You may feel an inexplicable sense of trust or unease, guiding your interactions and helping you navigate relationships with discernment and authenticity.

3. In creative pursuits, your intuition becomes a wellspring of inspiration. It guides you to explore unique ideas, take creative risks, and infuse your work with a sense of authenticity and originality. By embracing your intuitive flow, you tap into the limitless well of creative potential within you.

Intuition and gut feeling serve as gateways to our deepest knowing, transcending the limitations of logic and reason. By cultivating our intuitive senses, we embrace the art of listening to our inner voice, trusting its guidance, and aligning our actions with our highest truth.

Dear seekers of profound understanding, as we venture deeper into the realm of intuition and gut feeling, let us embrace the power of stillness, introspection, and mindful presence. Approach this practice with openness and receptivity, allowing your intuitive wisdom to unfold naturally. By nourishing your intuition, you empower yourself to make choices that resonate with your authentic self and lead to a life of purpose, fulfillment, and joy.

Technique 18 - Active Listening

In this chapter, we embark on a transformative exploration of the profound art of listening—one of the most potent tools for deepening connections, fostering understanding, and nurturing authentic relationships. Prepare to cultivate the invaluable skill of active listening, which opens the gateway to genuine communication, empathy, and profound connection with others.

Active listening, dear companions, is the practice of fully engaging with others by giving them our undivided attention, being fully present, and genuinely seeking to understand their words, emotions, and perspectives. It is a powerful act of empathy, where we create a safe and nurturing space for others to express themselves authentically. By mastering the art of active listening, we become catalysts for transformation, healing, and harmonious relationships.

Imagine, dear seekers, the immense power of active listening to bridge divides, dissolve conflicts, and cultivate profound understanding. By honing this skill, we move beyond surface-level conversations and tap into the rich tapestry of human experiences. We become beacons of compassion, offering solace, support, and validation to those who seek to be heard and understood.

Let us explore a tapestry of examples to illuminate the transformative nature of active listening:

1. Imagine a friend who is going through a challenging time. As they pour their heart out, actively listen by fully immersing yourself in their words, observing their body language, and acknowledging their emotions. By providing a safe space for their vulnerability, you offer

them solace, compassion, and the invaluable gift of being seen and heard.

2. In a professional setting, active listening enables you to understand the needs and desires of your colleagues or clients. By attentively absorbing their perspectives, you forge deeper connections, foster collaboration, and cultivate an environment where everyone's voice is valued.

3. In a family setting, active listening strengthens the bonds that hold loved ones together. By genuinely hearing the thoughts, concerns, and dreams of your family members, you nurture a sense of belonging, empathy, and understanding that enriches the tapestry of your shared experiences.

Active listening transcends mere hearing; it encompasses an intentional presence, an open heart, and a genuine desire to connect with others. It is an act of love, respect, and validation—a powerful tool for cultivating harmony, fostering empathy, and building bridges between diverse perspectives.

Dear seekers of profound understanding, as we delve deeper into the realm of active listening, let us embrace the power of silence, curiosity, and compassionate presence. Approach this practice with an open heart, shedding distractions and judgments. By mastering the art of active listening, we become vessels of healing, transformation, and authentic connection.

Technique 19 - Questioning Techniques

Welcome, dear seekers, to the illuminating realm of Questioning Techniques. In this chapter, we embark on a transformative exploration of the art of asking insightful questions—a powerful tool for expanding our understanding, gaining deeper insights, and uncovering hidden truths. Prepare to unleash the remarkable potential of questioning techniques as we delve into the realms of curiosity, self-reflection, and meaningful conversations.

Questioning, dear companions, is the art of crafting thoughtful inquiries that stimulate critical thinking, ignite curiosity, and invite introspection. It is a catalyst for growth, as it opens doorways to new perspectives, uncovers underlying motivations, and encourages self-discovery. By mastering the skill of questioning, we unlock the gateways to profound understanding, authentic connections, and personal transformation.

Imagine, dear seekers, the limitless possibilities that unfold when we embrace the power of asking meaningful questions. By channeling our curiosity, we embark on a journey of exploration, inviting others and ourselves to delve deeper into the layers of our thoughts, beliefs, and experiences. Through purposeful inquiry, we challenge assumptions, expand our horizons, and uncover the gems of wisdom hidden within.

Let us delve into the tapestry of examples to illuminate the transformative nature of questioning techniques:

1. In personal growth and self-reflection, asking powerful questions helps us uncover our core values, aspirations, and areas for growth. By

delving into the depths of our inner world, we gain clarity, direction, and a deeper understanding of ourselves.

2. In conversations and relationships, thoughtful questions create space for authentic connection and empathy. They allow us to truly see and understand others, fostering a sense of belonging, trust, and mutual respect.

3. In problem-solving and decision-making, well-crafted questions guide us to explore alternative perspectives, consider potential solutions, and challenge our limiting beliefs. They empower us to make informed choices and navigate life's challenges with clarity and intention.

Questioning techniques ignite the flame of curiosity, inviting us to embrace the mysteries of the world and our own existence. They facilitate meaningful conversations, unlock profound insights, and bridge gaps of understanding between diverse perspectives.

Dear seekers of profound understanding, as we venture deeper into the realm of questioning techniques, let us embrace the power of inquiry, active listening, and open-mindedness. Approach this practice with curiosity and humility, recognizing that each question holds the potential to illuminate new paths of growth and transformation.

Technique 20 - Building Rapport and Trust

Welcome, dear seekers, to the extraordinary realm of Building Rapport and Trust. In this chapter, we embark on a transformative exploration of the art of forging genuine connections, nurturing authentic relationships, and cultivating trust—a cornerstone of meaningful interactions and harmonious bonds. Prepare to unlock the remarkable potential of Technique 20 as we delve into the intricacies of rapport-building, empathetic communication, and the foundations of trust.

Building rapport, dear companions, is the sacred dance of creating a sense of familiarity, mutual understanding, and shared resonance with others. It is the delicate art of establishing a genuine connection that transcends surface-level interactions, allowing trust to blossom and relationships to flourish. By mastering the skill of building rapport, we pave the way for deep connections, collaboration, and authentic engagement.

Imagine, dear seekers, the profound impact that building rapport can have on our personal and professional lives. When we authentically connect with others, we create a space where vulnerability is welcomed, empathy is nurtured, and trust is fostered. Through rapport-building, we break down barriers, dissolve differences, and create a foundation for meaningful collaboration and collective growth.

Let us immerse ourselves in a tapestry of examples to illuminate the transformative nature of building rapport and trust:

1. In personal relationships, building rapport lays the groundwork for intimacy and understanding. By actively listening, expressing

empathy, and embracing vulnerability, we cultivate an environment where love, respect, and trust can thrive.

2. In professional settings, rapport-building becomes a catalyst for effective teamwork, collaboration, and innovation. When we connect authentically with colleagues, clients, and partners, we foster an atmosphere of mutual respect, open communication, and shared purpose.

3. In leadership and influence, building rapport allows us to connect deeply with others, inspiring trust, and influencing positive change. By understanding the unique perspectives and aspirations of those we lead, we create a sense of belonging, empowerment, and shared vision.

Building rapport requires genuine presence, empathy, and a willingness to embrace the beauty of human connection. It involves mirroring body language, establishing common ground, and expressing sincere interest in others' thoughts and experiences. By mastering this art, we become facilitators of understanding, compassion, and authentic engagement.

Dear seekers of profound connections, as we delve deeper into the realm of building rapport and trust, let us embrace the power of empathy, active listening, and vulnerability. Approach this practice with a genuine curiosity to understand and connect with others, recognizing that the seeds of trust are nurtured through authentic engagement and shared experiences.

Technique 21 - Empathic Listening

In this chapter, we embark on a transformative exploration of the art of truly hearing and understanding others—the essence of empathy and compassionate communication. Prepare to unlock the profound potential of Technique 21 as we delve into the intricacies of active listening, empathic presence, and the sacred dance of deep understanding.

Empathic listening, dear companions, is the noble practice of immersing ourselves fully in the experience of another. It is the art of listening not only with our ears but also with our hearts and souls, allowing us to connect deeply with the thoughts, emotions, and unspoken messages of those who grace our lives. By mastering the skill of empathic listening, we open the gateway to profound understanding, authentic connection, and transformative relationships.

Imagine, dear seekers, the power of truly listening to others without judgment or interruption. When we engage in empathic listening, we create a safe space for individuals to express their deepest truths, fears, and dreams. By holding this sacred space, we honor their experiences, validate their emotions, and offer solace and support. Through empathic listening, we foster healing, growth, and profound connection.

Let us immerse ourselves in a tapestry of examples to illuminate the transformative nature of empathic listening:

1. In personal relationships, empathic listening allows us to truly understand and connect with our loved ones. By offering our undivided attention, holding space for their joys and sorrows, and

listening with genuine curiosity, we deepen our bonds, nurture trust, and cultivate an atmosphere of unconditional love.

2. In conflict resolution, empathic listening becomes a bridge of understanding, paving the way for healing and reconciliation. By listening deeply to the perspectives of all parties involved, suspending judgment, and acknowledging their emotions, we create a space for dialogue, empathy, and finding common ground.

3. In leadership and coaching, empathic listening empowers us to guide and inspire others. By actively listening to the aspirations, challenges, and aspirations of those we lead, we foster a culture of belonging, growth, and shared purpose. Through empathic listening, we unlock the untapped potential within individuals and teams, igniting their passion and nurturing their growth.

Empathic listening requires us to be fully present, to quiet the noise of our own thoughts, and to offer our undivided attention to those who seek to be heard. It involves not just hearing the words spoken but also attuning ourselves to the underlying emotions, body language, and unspoken messages. By cultivating empathic listening, we become conduits of deep understanding, healing, and transformative connection.

Dear seekers of profound connections, as we venture deeper into the realm of empathic listening, let us embrace the power of presence, compassion, and the art of silence. Approach this practice with an open heart, a willingness to truly understand others, and a commitment to holding space for their experiences. Recognize that in the act of empathic listening, we honor the humanity, emotions, and unique journey of each individual.

Technique 22 - Mirror Neurons and Mimicry

In this chapter, we embark on a transformative exploration of the fascinating science behind our innate ability to mirror and mimic the behavior of others—a pathway to deep connection, empathy, and understanding. Prepare to unlock the profound potential of Technique 22 as we delve into the intricacies of mirror neurons, empathic resonance, and the art of subtle imitation.

Mirror neurons, dear companions, are the remarkable neural pathways within our brains that fire both when we perform an action and when we observe someone else performing the same action. They are the foundation of our capacity to empathize and connect with others on a profound level. By understanding the power of mirror neurons and harnessing the skill of intentional mimicry, we open the gateway to deep empathy, rapport, and harmonious relationships.

Imagine, dear seekers, the transformative impact of consciously mirroring the behavior, gestures, and expressions of another person. When we engage in this subtle dance of mimicry, we create an unconscious bond, a shared resonance that transcends words. By mirroring others, we signal our deep understanding and acceptance, fostering a sense of trust, connection, and unity.

Let us immerse ourselves in a tapestry of examples to illuminate the transformative nature of mirror neurons and mimicry:

1. In personal relationships, intentional mimicry allows us to establish a powerful connection with our loved ones. By mirroring their body language, tone of voice, and energy, we create a space of

familiarity and comfort. Through this subtle form of imitation, we communicate our understanding, empathy, and shared experience.

2. In professional settings, mimicry becomes a catalyst for collaboration, influence, and effective communication. By mirroring the behavior and communication style of our colleagues, clients, or partners, we establish a sense of rapport and create a foundation for shared understanding and productive teamwork.

3. In public speaking and presentations, intentional mimicry enables us to connect deeply with our audience. By subtly mirroring their nonverbal cues, we create a harmonious rhythm, engendering a sense of trust, and enhancing engagement. Through this unconscious imitation, we establish a bond of connection and captivate the hearts and minds of those we address.

Intentional mimicry requires us to attune ourselves to the subtle nuances of others' behavior, gestures, and energy. It involves mirroring their body language, facial expressions, and vocal patterns while maintaining authenticity and respect. By consciously utilizing mimicry as a tool for connection, we tap into the remarkable power of mirror neurons, creating a profound resonance with those we encounter.

Dear seekers of profound connections, as we journey deeper into the realm of mirror neurons and mimicry, let us embrace the power of observation, sensitivity, and intentionality. Approach this practice with genuine curiosity, empathy, and a genuine desire to understand and connect with others. Recognize that through conscious mimicry, we bridge the gap between individuals, fostering understanding, empathy, and profound connections.

Technique 23 - Contextualizing Verbal Communication

In this chapter, we embark on a transformative exploration of the intricate interplay between words, meaning, and the context in which they are spoken—a pathway to deeper understanding, effective communication, and harmonious relationships. Prepare to unlock the profound potential of Technique 23 as we delve into the art of decoding the layers of context within verbal interactions.

Verbal communication, dear companions, is a complex tapestry of words, tone, intention, and the context in which it unfolds. It is the currency through which we convey our thoughts, emotions, and desires. By understanding the power of contextualizing verbal communication, we gain insight into the hidden layers of meaning, nuances, and subtleties that shape our interactions.

Imagine, dear seekers, the transformative impact of consciously examining the context surrounding our conversations. When we engage in this nuanced practice of contextualizing verbal communication, we unravel the intricacies of intent, cultural nuances, and unspoken messages. By exploring the broader context, we gain a deeper understanding of the motives, values, and perspectives that influence our interactions.

Let us immerse ourselves in a tapestry of examples to illuminate the transformative nature of contextualizing verbal communication:

1. In personal relationships, contextualizing verbal communication enables us to connect on a deeper level. By considering the circumstances, emotions, and past experiences that influence the

conversation, we develop empathy, understanding, and the ability to respond in a way that fosters connection and support.

2. In professional settings, contextualizing verbal communication becomes a catalyst for effective collaboration and leadership. By taking into account the organizational culture, power dynamics, and individual backgrounds, we navigate complex conversations with skill and sensitivity, fostering trust, and driving meaningful outcomes.

3. In intercultural communication, contextualizing verbal communication helps bridge the gaps between different perspectives and worldviews. By considering cultural norms, values, and beliefs, we navigate potential misunderstandings, promote inclusivity, and cultivate authentic connections across diverse communities.

Contextualizing verbal communication requires us to go beyond the surface level of words and actively engage with the broader context. It involves considering the environment, nonverbal cues, the relationship dynamics, and the underlying emotions that shape the conversation. By cultivating this awareness, we develop the ability to listen, respond, and adapt with empathy, grace, and authenticity.

Dear seekers of meaningful connections, as we venture deeper into the realm of contextualizing verbal communication, let us embrace the power of active listening, curiosity, and cultural sensitivity. Approach this practice with an open mind, a willingness to learn, and a genuine desire to understand the rich tapestry of context that colors our conversations. Recognize that by contextualizing verbal communication, we transcend mere words, fostering deeper connections, and nurturing harmonious relationships.

Technique 24 - Nonverbal Synchrony

Welcome, dear seekers, to the captivating realm of Nonverbal Synchrony. In this chapter, we embark on a transformative exploration of the intricate dance of nonverbal cues—the unspoken language that profoundly shapes our interactions and connections. Prepare to unlock the profound potential of Technique 24 as we delve into the art of nonverbal synchrony, the power of subtle mirroring, and the transformative impact it has on our relationships.

Nonverbal communication, dear companions, is a tapestry of gestures, facial expressions, body language, and energy that transcends words. It is the language of connection, understanding, and unspoken resonance. By understanding the power of nonverbal synchrony and harnessing the skill of intentional mirroring, we create a profound sense of unity, trust, and rapport.

Imagine, dear seekers, the transformative impact of synchronizing our nonverbal cues with those around us. When we engage in this subtle dance of nonverbal synchrony, we establish a deep and intuitive connection. Through mirroring the gestures, body language, and energy of others, we create a sense of shared experience, understanding, and trust.

Nonverbal synchrony is the art of aligning our nonverbal cues with those of our conversation partners. It involves mirroring their gestures, body posture, facial expressions, and even their breathing patterns. By consciously engaging in nonverbal synchrony, we create a seamless connection, a dance of resonance that transcends words and fosters a profound sense of connection and understanding.

Let us immerse ourselves in a tapestry of examples to illuminate the transformative nature of nonverbal synchrony:

1. In personal relationships, nonverbal synchrony allows us to establish a deep and intuitive connection with our loved ones. By mirroring their body language, facial expressions, and energy, we create a safe and harmonious space. Through this unspoken mirroring, we communicate our understanding, empathy, and shared emotional experience.

2. In professional settings, nonverbal synchrony becomes a catalyst for effective communication, collaboration, and leadership. By mirroring the nonverbal cues of our colleagues, clients, or team members, we establish a sense of rapport and create a foundation for trust, cooperation, and shared goals. Through this synchronized dance, we enhance our ability to influence, inspire, and create meaningful connections.

3. In public speaking and presentations, nonverbal synchrony enables us to connect deeply with our audience. By aligning our gestures, body language, and energy with that of the audience, we establish a powerful resonance. Through this intentional mirroring, we create a sense of unity, captivate attention, and evoke a profound emotional response.

Nonverbal synchrony requires us to be attentive, present, and attuned to the cues of our conversation partners. It involves listening not only with our ears but also with our whole being, observing the subtleties of body language, energy, and nonverbal expressions. By consciously engaging in nonverbal synchrony, we bridge the gap between individuals, fostering understanding, empathy, and profound connections.

Dear seekers of profound connections, as we journey deeper into the realm of nonverbal synchrony, let us embrace the power of observation, empathy, and intentionality. Approach this practice with genuine curiosity, respect, and a genuine desire to connect and understand others. Recognize that through nonverbal synchrony, we create a harmonious dance of connection and foster transformative relationships.

Technique 25 - Subtle Linguistic Cues

Dear fellow seekers, welcome to the enlightening realm of Technique 25 - Subtle Linguistic Cues. In this chapter, we embark on a profound exploration of the hidden gems concealed within the words we choose, the tone we employ, and the nuances we convey through our language. Prepare to unlock the transformative power of linguistic cues as we delve into the art of decoding subtle signals, understanding deeper meanings, and cultivating authentic connections.

Language, dear companions, is not solely a means of communication but a window into the depths of our thoughts, emotions, and motivations. It is through the careful examination of linguistic cues that we unravel the hidden truths, untangle the layers of meaning, and gain profound insights into the minds and hearts of others.

Technique 25 invites us to become astute observers of the subtle linguistic cues woven into our everyday conversations. These cues manifest themselves in the choice of words, sentence structures, vocal inflections, and even pauses between spoken words. By attuning ourselves to these delicate linguistic signals, we gain a deeper understanding of the unspoken narratives, desires, and emotions underlying the surface level of communication.

Let us immerse ourselves in a tapestry of examples to illuminate the transformative nature of subtle linguistic cues:

1. In personal relationships, paying attention to the subtle linguistic cues helps us decipher the underlying emotions and desires of our loved ones. By noticing the shifts in tone, word choices, and

nonverbal cues during a conversation, we gain insights into their true feelings and needs. Through this understanding, we foster empathy, strengthen emotional connections, and cultivate harmonious relationships.

2. In professional interactions, recognizing and interpreting subtle linguistic cues empowers us to navigate complex dynamics with finesse and insight. By carefully listening to the choice of words, the tone of voice, and the level of conviction in the speaker's delivery, we gain a deeper understanding of their perspective, motivations, and intentions. Through this heightened awareness, we build trust, resolve conflicts, and enhance collaboration.

3. In public speaking and persuasive communication, utilizing subtle linguistic cues allows us to engage and influence our audience more effectively. By employing rhetorical devices, word choices, and pacing that resonate with the values and aspirations of the listeners, we create a powerful connection and inspire action. Through this skillful orchestration of language, we ignite minds, stir emotions, and foster transformative change.

The art of decoding subtle linguistic cues requires us to be present, attentive, and attuned to the intricate dance of words. It involves active listening, empathetic understanding, and an insatiable curiosity to uncover the deeper meanings beneath the surface. By honing our skills in deciphering linguistic cues, we embark on a journey of profound connection, authentic communication, and enriched relationships.

Dear seekers of authentic connections, as we venture deeper into the realm of subtle linguistic cues, let us embrace the power of attentive listening, empathetic interpretation, and genuine curiosity. Approach this practice with an open heart, a discerning mind, and a commitment to fostering genuine connections. Recognize that through the mastery of linguistic cues, we transcend superficial communication, unlocking the doors to profound understanding and authentic relationships.

In the next chapter, we will explore Technique 26, an illuminating method for deciphering the subconscious messages hidden within metaphorical language. Get ready to unravel the metaphorical tapestry and gain deeper insights into the thoughts, beliefs, and desires of others.

Technique 26 - Analyzing Microexpressions in Conversations

In this chapter, we embark on a fascinating journey into the realm of microexpressions, those fleeting and involuntary facial expressions that reveal the true emotions concealed beneath the surface. Prepare to delve into the intricacies of nonverbal communication, as we learn to decipher the unspoken language of the face.

Dear friends, it is said that the eyes are the windows to the soul. In Technique 26, we focus our attention on these portals of truth, where fleeting microexpressions flash across the face, revealing authentic emotions that words alone cannot express. By developing our skills in analyzing and interpreting these microexpressions, we gain profound insights into the thoughts, feelings, and intentions of those around us.

Let us journey together through a tapestry of examples that illustrate the power and significance of microexpressions in conversations:

1. During a negotiation, a slight raise of an eyebrow or a fleeting microexpression of surprise may hint at a hidden agenda or a concealed intention. By keenly observing these subtle facial movements, we can navigate the negotiation with heightened awareness, understanding the unspoken dynamics and making informed decisions.

2. In personal relationships, the ability to decode microexpressions enables us to truly connect with others at a deeper level. When engaged in a heartfelt conversation, the flicker of joy, the tinge of sadness, or the hint of anxiety can provide valuable cues about the emotional state of our loved ones. By attentively noticing and empathetically responding

to these microexpressions, we cultivate stronger bonds and foster emotional intimacy.

3. In leadership and management, the skill of analyzing microexpressions grants us valuable insights into the emotions and reactions of our team members. By observing microexpressions of frustration, confusion, or enthusiasm, we can tailor our communication and leadership style to address their needs effectively. This heightened understanding allows us to build trust, inspire motivation, and create an environment that fosters growth and productivity.

Analyzing microexpressions is an art that requires both patience and practice. It involves cultivating a keen eye for subtle facial movements, mastering the art of attentive observation, and developing a deep sense of empathy. By honing these skills, we become skilled interpreters of the nonverbal symphony, harmonizing the language of the face with the words spoken.

Dear seekers of truth, as we venture into the realm of microexpressions, let us approach this practice with humility, curiosity, and a genuine desire to connect with others at a profound level. Recognize that analyzing microexpressions is not about manipulation or deception but about fostering authentic connections and understanding. Through this practice, we enhance our ability to communicate effectively, build trust, and forge meaningful relationships.

Technique 27 - Detecting Deception

In this chapter, we embark on a riveting exploration of uncovering the veiled truths and hidden intentions concealed within human communication. Prepare to sharpen your discernment and hone your investigative skills as we delve into the art of detecting deception.

Dear friends, deception is an intricate dance, where words can become masks, and actions can veil true intentions. In a world where dishonesty can infiltrate our interactions, Technique 27 equips us with the tools to navigate the treacherous waters of deception, allowing us to chart a course towards genuine authenticity and trust.

Let us embark on a transformative journey together, weaving through a tapestry of examples that illuminate the art of detecting deception in various contexts:

1. Personal Relationships: In the realm of personal relationships, trust is the foundation that binds souls together. By mastering the skill of detecting deception, we empower ourselves to recognize the subtle discrepancies between words and actions, the fleeting microexpressions that betray hidden emotions, and the inconsistencies in stories that reveal the presence of deceit. Through this heightened awareness, we safeguard our hearts and cultivate relationships rooted in authenticity and integrity.

For example, imagine a scenario where a friend repeatedly cancels plans with vague excuses. By discerning the incongruence between their words and actions, we may begin to question the authenticity of their intentions. Through compassionate communication and honest dialogue, we can address these concerns and forge stronger connections based on trust and openness.

2. Professional Settings: In the realm of work and business, the ability to detect deception is a valuable asset. It allows us to navigate negotiations, detect dishonest practices, and make informed decisions. By honing our skills in analyzing nonverbal cues, deciphering hidden agendas, and evaluating the consistency of information, we become adept at uncovering deceptive tactics and protecting our interests.

For instance, imagine a high-stakes business negotiation where both parties present seemingly attractive proposals. By keenly observing body language, vocal intonations, and subtle shifts in demeanor, we can uncover signs of deceit or manipulation. Armed with this knowledge, we can approach the negotiation with a balanced perspective and make decisions that align with our best interests.

3. Media and Information Consumption: In the era of abundant information, the ability to detect deception becomes crucial for discerning truth from misinformation. By employing critical thinking, fact-checking, and analyzing the credibility of sources, we shield ourselves from falling victim to manipulation or propaganda. We become responsible consumers of information, adept at sifting through the noise to uncover the nuggets of truth.

For instance, imagine encountering a news article that presents sensational claims without credible evidence. By applying the principles of detecting deception, we scrutinize the sources, evaluate the consistency of information across different platforms, and question the underlying motivations behind the narrative. This discernment allows us to form well-informed opinions and contribute to meaningful conversations.

Detecting deception is a multidimensional skill that encompasses keen observation, emotional intelligence, and critical thinking. It involves deciphering the nuances of nonverbal communication, analyzing verbal cues, and trusting our intuition. However, it is essential to approach this practice with integrity, empathy, and a commitment to ethical communication. The goal is not to become cynics but to foster authentic connections and preserve the essence of truth.

Dear seekers of truth, as we delve into the depths of detecting deception, let us embrace this journey with a profound understanding of its impact on our lives. By sharpening our ability to recognize deceit, we become guardians of authenticity, promoting trust, and fostering genuine connections. Through this practice, we not only protect ourselves but also contribute to a world where truth prevails.

Technique 28 - Reading Emotional States in Others

In this chapter, we embark on an illuminating journey through the intricate landscapes of human emotions. Prepare to deepen your understanding of the human experience as we unravel the subtle cues and signals that reveal the emotional states of those around us.

Dear friends, emotions are the vibrant colors that paint the tapestry of our lives. They hold immense power to shape our interactions, relationships, and overall well-being. Technique 28 invites us to become skilled observers, attuned to the emotional currents that flow beneath the surface. Through this practice, we develop an empathetic lens, enabling us to forge deeper connections, offer support, and navigate the complex web of human emotions with grace and understanding.

Let us embark on this transformative journey together, exploring the vast spectrum of emotions and uncovering the profound insights they hold:

1. Recognizing Facial Expressions: The human face is a canvas upon which emotions are artfully displayed. By honing our ability to read facial expressions, we unlock a wealth of information about the inner emotional landscape of others. From a joyful smile that radiates warmth to a furrowed brow signaling concern, each facial expression carries a unique story waiting to be discovered. Through careful observation, we become adept at deciphering the nuanced microexpressions that flicker across the face, revealing glimpses of underlying emotions.

For example, imagine encountering a colleague who, despite wearing a cheerful mask, exhibits subtle signs of sadness in their eyes. By attuning ourselves to these cues, we can extend compassion, offer support, and create a safe space for open dialogue, fostering an environment of emotional well-being.

2. Interpreting Body Language: The body is a powerful communicator, silently expressing emotions through its postures, gestures, and movements. By reading body language, we gain insights into the unspoken messages that lie within. The crossed arms that signify defensiveness, the slumped shoulders indicating sadness, or the open and relaxed posture that exudes confidence—all contribute to the intricate tapestry of emotional states. By paying attention to these subtle cues, we become skilled interpreters of the language of the body.

For instance, imagine attending a networking event where you notice someone exhibiting closed-off body language, avoiding eye contact, and displaying fidgety movements. These cues might suggest discomfort or unease. By recognizing these signals, we can approach the individual with empathy, creating a safe space for them to share their feelings and fostering a connection rooted in understanding.

3. Listening Beyond Words: Verbal communication is just one facet of expression, often accompanied by a deeper emotional undercurrent. By listening beyond the words spoken, we uncover the nuances of tone, inflection, and pauses that reveal the true emotional states of others. Through active listening and attunement to the subtleties of vocal cues, we develop a heightened sensitivity to the underlying emotions conveyed through speech.

For instance, imagine a friend sharing their recent achievements with a tone that lacks enthusiasm or carries a tinge of self-doubt. By attuning ourselves to these vocal cues, we can offer genuine encouragement, acknowledge their journey, and provide the support they may need, beyond the surface-level narrative.

4. Sensing Energy and Vibes: Beyond the observable cues, every individual emits a unique energy or vibe—an intangible force that conveys their emotional state. By cultivating our intuitive senses, we tap into this energetic realm, perceiving the emotional undercurrents that swirl around us. This heightened sensitivity allows us to navigate social dynamics, detect shifts in moods, and extend empathy without words.

For instance, imagine entering a room where the atmosphere feels heavy with tension, even though no one has spoken a word

. By attuning ourselves to the energy present, we can respond with kindness, compassion, and a genuine desire to alleviate the underlying emotional burden, fostering a more harmonious environment for all.

Dear seekers of emotional connection, as we deepen our understanding of reading emotional states in others, let us approach this practice with humility, empathy, and a commitment to respecting boundaries. It is not about manipulating or intruding upon the emotions of others, but rather about fostering authentic connections, offering support, and creating spaces where emotional well-being can flourish.

Technique 29 - Uncovering Subconscious Motivations

Welcome, dear explorers of the human psyche, to Technique 29 - Uncovering Subconscious Motivations. In this chapter, we delve into the depths of the human mind, peering beyond the conscious thoughts and actions to unravel the hidden drivers that shape our behavior. Prepare to embark on a captivating journey of self-discovery and understanding as we explore the intricacies of our subconscious motivations.

Dear friends, within the recesses of our minds lie a myriad of desires, fears, and aspirations that influence our every move, often operating outside the realm of conscious awareness. Technique 29 invites us to shine a light on these elusive forces, unveiling the underlying motivations that propel our actions and decisions. Through this practice, we gain profound insights into ourselves and others, fostering empathy, connection, and personal growth.

Let us embark on this enlightening expedition, as we uncover the layers of subconscious motivations and unlock a deeper understanding of human behavior:

1. Exploring Core Values: Our values serve as guiding principles that shape our choices and actions. By exploring our core values and those of others, we gain a glimpse into the subconscious motivations driving our behavior. Whether it's a relentless pursuit of justice, a yearning for personal growth, or a deep-seated need for connection, our core values can reveal the underlying reasons behind our decisions and actions.

For example, imagine a friend who consistently prioritizes giving back to the community and supporting social causes. By understanding their core value of compassion and making a positive impact, we can better comprehend their choices and extend support that aligns with their underlying motivations.

2. Uncovering Childhood Imprints: Our experiences in childhood leave imprints on our subconscious minds, shaping our beliefs, fears, and desires. By exploring the influences of our early years, we gain insights into the subconscious motivations that drive our behavior today. Understanding how childhood experiences have shaped our perception of the world allows us to approach ourselves and others with empathy and compassion.

For instance, consider someone who grew up in an environment where they were constantly criticized. This experience may have shaped their subconscious motivation for seeking validation and approval. By recognizing this underlying drive, we can foster an environment that nurtures their sense of self-worth and supports their personal growth.

3. Examining Emotional Triggers: Emotions act as powerful catalysts, often steering our actions and decisions without our conscious awareness. By examining our emotional triggers and those of others, we gain a deeper understanding of the subconscious motivations that arise in response to certain situations. Whether it's fear, insecurity, or a desire for control, our emotional triggers hold valuable clues to the underlying motivations that influence our behavior.

For example, suppose a colleague consistently becomes defensive and confrontational during team meetings. By recognizing that their behavior may be triggered by a fear of being criticized or a deep-rooted need for validation, we can approach them with empathy, creating a safe space for open communication and collaboration.

4. Analyzing Patterns and Habits: Our habits and patterns of behavior often hold clues to our subconscious motivations. By

analyzing these repetitive behaviors, we can uncover the underlying drivers that perpetuate them. Whether it's a pattern of procrastination, seeking constant validation, or avoiding conflict, recognizing these patterns allows us to address the root causes and make conscious choices that align with our true desires.

For instance, consider someone who repeatedly finds themselves in toxic relationships. By examining the patterns and uncovering the subconscious motivations driving their choices, they can break free from unhealthy cycles and cultivate relationships that align with their values and aspirations.

Dear seekers of self-awareness and understanding, as we delve into the realm of uncovering subconscious motivations, let us approach this practice with curiosity, compassion, and a commitment to personal growth. It is not

about dissecting ourselves or others, but rather about gaining a deeper awareness of the forces that shape our lives and the lives of those around us.

In the next chapter, Technique 30, we will explore the power of visualization and how it can help us tap into our subconscious mind to unlock our true potential. Get ready to harness the incredible power of your imagination as we embark on this transformative journey of self-discovery.

Remember, dear friends, the pursuit of understanding our subconscious motivations is a lifelong endeavor. With each discovery, we inch closer to aligning our actions with our authentic selves, fostering deeper connections, and embracing the fullness of our human experience.

Technique 30 - Identifying Hidden Agendas

Welcome, dear seekers of truth, to Technique 30 - Identifying Hidden Agendas. In this chapter, we delve into the intricate dance of human interactions, peering beyond the surface level to uncover the hidden agendas that often lie beneath. Prepare to sharpen your discernment and deepen your understanding of the intentions and motives that shape our interactions.

Dear friends, as we navigate the complex tapestry of human relationships, it is essential to recognize that not everything is as it seems. Behind the words, gestures, and actions, hidden agendas may be at play, driving individuals towards specific outcomes or hidden desires. Technique 30 invites us to develop a keen sense of perception and discernment, enabling us to uncover these hidden agendas and gain a more comprehensive understanding of the dynamics at play.

Let us embark on this illuminating exploration, as we unravel the secrets of hidden agendas:

1. Observing Inconsistencies: Hidden agendas often reveal themselves through inconsistencies in words, actions, or body language. By keenly observing these discrepancies, we can start to discern the underlying motives behind someone's behavior. Pay attention to moments when what is said does not align with what is shown, as these inconsistencies can be valuable clues to hidden agendas.

For example, imagine a situation where a coworker consistently praises a colleague in public but subtly undermines them in private conversations. By recognizing the inconsistency between their public praise and private actions, we can begin to uncover their hidden agenda of gaining favor and exerting control.

2. Noticing Selective Information Sharing: Hidden agendas may involve strategic information withholding or selective sharing to shape others' perceptions or outcomes. By paying attention to what information is shared or withheld, we can gain insights into someone's hidden motives. Look for patterns of selective disclosure, and consider the underlying reasons behind these choices.

For instance, suppose a friend only shares positive aspects of their life on social media while consistently downplaying or omitting any challenges they face. This selective information sharing may stem from a hidden agenda to maintain a specific image or garner validation and admiration from others.

3. Understanding Power Dynamics: Hidden agendas often thrive within power dynamics, where individuals seek to maintain control or influence over others. By analyzing the power dynamics at play in a given situation, we can better discern hidden agendas and the motives driving certain behaviors. Pay attention to situations where power imbalances exist, and consider how these imbalances may impact the hidden agendas at play.

For example, in a corporate setting, a manager may exhibit a hidden agenda of promoting their own interests by stifling the ideas and contributions of their subordinates. Recognizing the power dynamics at play can help us navigate such situations with greater insight and empathy.

4. Trusting Your Intuition: Our intuition serves as a powerful compass when it comes to detecting hidden agendas. By honing our intuition and trusting our gut feelings, we can sense when something feels off or incongruent in a given interaction. Cultivate self-awareness and attune yourself to the subtle signals that your intuition sends, guiding you towards a deeper understanding of hidden motives.

For instance, suppose you meet someone for the first time, and despite their friendly demeanor, your intuition sends subtle signals of caution. Trusting your intuition may allow you to uncover their hidden agenda, ensuring your well-being and protecting yourself from potential harm.

Dear seekers of truth and discernment, as we navigate the complexities of hidden agendas, let us approach this practice with humility, empathy, and a commitment to fostering authentic connections. Uncovering hidden agendas is not about judgment or manipulation, but rather about gaining a deeper understanding of the dynamics at play and navigating our interactions with wisdom and grace.

In the next chapter, Technique 31, we will explore the power of effective communication and how it can strengthen our relationships and minimize the influence of hidden agendas. Get ready to delve into the art of clear and conscious communication, as we equip ourselves with invaluable tools for creating meaningful connections.

Remember, dear friends, the path of understanding and unraveling hidden agendas is not about manipulation or deceit but about fostering authentic connections and embracing the truth. With each technique we explore, we deepen our capacity for insight, empathy, and meaningful relationships.

Stay committed to the journey of mind reading, dear friends, as we continue to unravel the mysteries that lie beneath the surface. May this chapter inspire you to cultivate a discerning eye and an open heart as you navigate the intricate dance of human interactions.

Technique 31 - Analyzing Emotional Triggers

Welcome, dear seekers of self-awareness, to Technique 31 - Analyzing Emotional Triggers. In this chapter, we embark on a profound exploration of our emotional landscapes, diving into the depths of our inner world to unravel the intricacies of our emotional triggers. Prepare to embark on a transformative journey of self-discovery, as we learn to decode the messages hidden within our emotional responses.

Dear friends, our emotions hold profound wisdom and provide valuable insights into our inner workings. Technique 31 invites us to develop a heightened awareness of our emotional triggers, those powerful catalysts that ignite emotional responses within us. By analyzing these triggers, we gain a deeper understanding of ourselves and others, fostering greater empathy, compassion, and emotional intelligence.

Let us embark on this enlightening journey of emotional exploration, as we uncover the secrets of emotional triggers:

1. Recognizing Patterns: Emotional triggers often arise from recurring patterns in our lives. By observing these patterns, we can identify the common themes or situations that tend to elicit strong emotional reactions within us. Pay attention to the circumstances, events, or interactions that consistently provoke intense emotional responses, as these can serve as valuable entry points for self-reflection.

For example, imagine finding yourself consistently reacting with anger whenever someone challenges your beliefs or questions your competence. By recognizing this recurring pattern, you can delve deeper into the underlying insecurities or fears that may be triggered in these situations.

2. Uncovering Past Wounds: Emotional triggers often stem from unresolved past experiences or traumas. These unresolved wounds act as sensitized areas within us, easily activated by certain stimuli or situations. By exploring our past with curiosity and compassion, we can shed light on the origin of our emotional triggers, allowing for healing and growth.

For instance, suppose a seemingly innocuous comment from a friend triggers intense feelings of abandonment within you. Through self-reflection and perhaps therapy or counseling, you may discover that this trigger connects back to past experiences of feeling abandoned or neglected.

3. Examining Core Beliefs: Our core beliefs, deeply ingrained within us, significantly influence our emotional triggers. By examining our core beliefs and how they shape our perceptions, we can uncover the underlying beliefs that fuel our emotional reactions. Question the beliefs you hold about yourself, others, and the world, and consider how these beliefs contribute to your emotional triggers.

For example, if you have a core belief that you are unworthy of love and acceptance, any perceived rejection or criticism may trigger intense feelings of unworthiness or shame.

4. Practicing Mindful Awareness: Cultivating mindful awareness allows us to observe our emotional triggers with non-judgmental curiosity. By becoming fully present in the moment, we can notice the physical sensations, thoughts, and emotions that arise when triggered. Embrace a gentle, compassionate stance toward yourself as you explore these triggers, allowing for greater self-understanding and growth.

For instance, when you notice an emotional trigger arising, take a moment to pause, breathe, and observe the sensations and thoughts that accompany it. By cultivating this mindful awareness, you create space for reflection and conscious choice in how you respond.

Dear seekers of emotional wisdom, as we navigate the intricate landscape of emotional triggers, let us approach this practice with gentleness, patience, and a commitment to self-compassion. Analyzing emotional triggers is not about suppressing or avoiding our emotions but about understanding their origins and gaining mastery over our responses.

Technique 32 - Identifying Manipulative Tactics

Dear seekers of truth and discernment, welcome to Technique 32 - Identifying Manipulative Tactics. In this chapter, we embark on a crucial journey of awareness, where we learn to recognize and understand the manipulative tactics that can hinder our personal growth, relationships, and overall well-being. Armed with this knowledge, we can navigate the intricate webs of manipulation with clarity and integrity.

Manipulation is a subtle art, often disguised behind a veil of charm, persuasion, or coercion. Technique 32 invites us to sharpen our senses, develop our intuition, and cultivate a discerning mind. By familiarizing ourselves with common manipulative tactics, we gain the power to protect ourselves and others from their detrimental effects.

Let us delve into the realm of manipulation, unveiling its deceptive nature and empowering ourselves with knowledge:

1. Gaslighting: Gaslighting is a manipulative tactic that seeks to distort someone's perception of reality, making them question their own thoughts, emotions, and memories. Manipulators may deny or downplay their harmful actions, make the victim doubt their sanity, or shift blame onto them. By recognizing gaslighting tactics, we can reclaim our truth and protect our mental and emotional well-being.

For example, if someone consistently undermines your experiences or dismisses your emotions, making you doubt your own reality, it could be a sign of gaslighting.

2. Guilt-Tripping: Guilt-tripping is a tactic used to manipulate others by eliciting feelings of guilt or obligation. Manipulators may

employ emotional manipulation, exaggerated victimhood, or subtle emotional blackmail to coerce compliance or gain an upper hand. By understanding guilt-tripping techniques, we can set healthy boundaries and make choices aligned with our own values and well-being.

For instance, if someone repeatedly tries to make you feel guilty for prioritizing your own needs or boundaries, it may be a form of guilt-tripping.

3. Love-Bombing: Love-bombing is a manipulation tactic often employed in romantic relationships or by charismatic individuals seeking control. Manipulators shower their targets with excessive attention, affection, and flattery to create dependency and weaken their boundaries. Recognizing love-bombing tactics empowers us to discern genuine love and build healthy, balanced relationships.

For example, if someone rapidly escalates the intensity of a relationship, overwhelming you with affection and grand gestures early on, it may be a sign of love-bombing.

4. Manipulative Language: Manipulators often use language to influence, deceive, or control others. This can include tactics such as persuasive speech, loaded questions, subtle threats, or withholding information. By developing awareness of manipulative language patterns, we can maintain clarity of thought, assert our boundaries, and communicate authentically.

For instance, if someone consistently uses vague language, avoids direct answers, or resorts to personal attacks during discussions, they may be using manipulative language to undermine your position or control the narrative.

5. Emotional Manipulation: Emotional manipulation involves manipulating others' emotions to gain control or advantage. This can include tactics like playing the victim, using emotional outbursts to guilt or intimidate, or employing emotional manipulation to elicit specific reactions. By recognizing emotional manipulation techniques, we can protect our emotional well-being and make informed choices.

For example, if someone consistently uses emotional manipulation to make you feel responsible for their happiness or to avoid taking accountability for their actions, it is important to recognize and address this manipulation.

Dear seekers of truth and empowerment, by becoming adept at identifying manipulative tactics, we reclaim our autonomy, protect our boundaries, and cultivate healthy relationships based on authenticity and trust. Remember, the power to recognize manipulation lies within you, and as you refine your discernment, you can create a reality rooted in truth and genuine connections.

Technique 33 - Emotional Calibration

In this chapter, we embark on a transformative journey of understanding and harnessing the power of our emotions. By developing the skill of emotional calibration, we unlock the key to navigating our inner landscape and forging deeper connections with ourselves and others.

Emotions are the intricate threads that weave the tapestry of our human experience. They are the messengers of our deepest desires, fears, and aspirations. Technique 33 invites us to embark on a profound exploration of our emotional realm, guiding us toward a heightened sense of self-awareness and emotional mastery.

Let us dive into the realms of emotional calibration, where we learn to:

1. Recognize and Identify Emotions: Emotions are like colors that paint the canvas of our lives. In this section, we will learn to identify and name the wide spectrum of emotions that flow through us. By cultivating awareness of our emotional landscape, we gain the power to navigate our internal experiences with clarity and understanding.

For example, we might distinguish between subtle nuances like sadness, grief, or melancholy, allowing us to honor and address these emotions with compassion.

2. Understand Emotional Triggers: Our emotions often act as guiding lights, illuminating areas of growth and healing within us. In this section, we will explore the roots of our emotional triggers and understand how past experiences shape our emotional responses in the present. By unraveling the layers of our triggers, we can cultivate empathy, forgiveness, and personal growth.

For instance, we might discover that certain situations or words trigger unresolved wounds from our past, allowing us to respond with greater compassion and awareness.

3. Cultivate Emotional Balance: Emotions are neither good nor bad; they are simply messengers. In this section, we will explore practices and techniques to cultivate emotional balance. We will learn how to embrace the full range of our emotions, allowing them to flow through us without being overwhelmed or controlled by them. By embracing emotional balance, we find inner peace and resilience amidst life's challenges.

For example, we might explore mindfulness techniques that help us observe our emotions without judgment, allowing them to naturally arise and dissipate.

4. Empathize and Connect: Emotions are a universal language that binds us all. In this section, we will delve into the art of empathy, deepening our ability to understand and connect with the emotions of others. By honing our empathic skills, we foster authentic connections, strengthen relationships, and create a more compassionate world.

For instance, we might practice active listening, tuning in to both verbal and nonverbal cues, allowing us to truly understand and validate the emotions expressed by others.

5. Harness Emotions for Growth: Emotions hold immense wisdom and transformative power. In this section, we will explore how to harness our emotions as catalysts for personal growth and positive change. By embracing the lessons embedded within our emotional experiences, we can transform challenges into opportunities for self-discovery, resilience, and self-actualization.

Technique 34 - Empathy Mapping

Dear compassionate souls on the path of emotional intelligence and deep connection, welcome to Technique 34 - Empathy Mapping. In this chapter, we embark on a transformative exploration of understanding and fostering empathy, a powerful force that binds us as humans and nurtures authentic relationships.

Empathy is the art of truly seeing and understanding others, stepping into their shoes, and embracing their experiences with an open heart and mind. Technique 34 invites us to delve into the realm of empathy mapping, a practice that allows us to cultivate deeper connections and forge pathways of understanding with those around us.

Let us dive into the realms of empathy mapping, where we will:

1. Cultivate Curiosity and Openness: Empathy starts with a genuine curiosity and willingness to understand others. In this section, we will explore the art of active listening and observing, learning to suspend judgment and embrace a mindset of openness. By cultivating curiosity, we create a safe space for others to share their stories and emotions.

For instance, we might engage in meaningful conversations, asking open-ended questions that invite others to share their thoughts and feelings.

2. Practice Perspective-Taking: Empathy is the ability to step into someone else's shoes and view the world from their perspective. In this section, we will learn techniques for perspective-taking, expanding our awareness beyond our own experiences. By immersing ourselves

in different viewpoints, we develop a deeper understanding of the complex tapestry of human experiences.

For example, we might engage in role-playing exercises, imagining ourselves in someone else's situation and considering their thoughts, feelings, and motivations.

3. Listen with Empathy: Listening is a powerful act of empathy. In this section, we will explore empathic listening techniques that allow us to truly hear and validate others' emotions and experiences. By listening with empathy, we create a space for others to express themselves authentically and feel heard and understood.

For instance, we might practice reflective listening, paraphrasing what others have shared to show that we genuinely grasp their perspective.

4. Recognize and Validate Emotions: Emotions lie at the core of human experiences, and empathy involves acknowledging and validating these emotions. In this section, we will learn to recognize and empathize with a wide range of emotions expressed by others. By honoring and validating their emotions, we foster a sense of safety and trust.

For example, we might say, "I can see that you're feeling frustrated right now. It must be challenging for you."

5. Connect Through Shared Humanity: Empathy reminds us of our shared humanity, the common thread that unites us all. In this section, we will explore how to connect on a deeper level by finding common ground with others. By recognizing our shared experiences, struggles, and aspirations, we bridge the gaps between us and build bridges of understanding.

For instance, we might share personal stories or experiences that resonate with others' challenges or triumphs, creating a sense of camaraderie and connection.

6. Cultivate Empathy in Action: Empathy becomes transformative when translated into action. In this section, we will explore how to

channel empathy into compassionate actions that make a positive impact on the lives of others. By taking tangible steps to support and uplift those around us, we foster a culture of empathy and kindness.

For example, we might volunteer for a cause that aligns with someone's struggles or offer a helping hand to someone in need.

Dear empathetic souls, as we embark on this journey of empathy mapping, let us embrace the beauty of human connection and the transformative power of understanding. Through empathy, we create bridges of compassion and build a world where everyone feels seen, heard, and valued.

Technique 35 - Building Emotional Connections

Dear seekers of meaningful connections and deep emotional bonds, welcome to Technique 35 - Building Emotional Connections. In this chapter, we embark on a transformative exploration of fostering authentic and profound connections with others, nurturing relationships that enrich our lives and bring us profound joy.

Building emotional connections goes beyond surface-level interactions. It involves creating a safe and nurturing space where vulnerability, empathy, and understanding flourish. Technique 35 invites us to cultivate the skills and mindset needed to forge deep emotional connections with the people who matter most to us.

In this chapter, we will embark on a journey of connection and learn how to:

1. Cultivate Emotional Availability: Building emotional connections starts with being emotionally available ourselves. In this section, we will explore the importance of being present, attentive, and open-hearted in our interactions. By cultivating emotional availability, we create an environment where others feel comfortable sharing their thoughts, feelings, and experiences.

For instance, we might practice active listening, putting aside distractions and giving our full attention to the person we are engaging with.

2. Create a Safe and Non-Judgmental Space: Emotional connections thrive in an environment free from judgment and criticism. In this section, we will learn how to create a safe and

non-judgmental space for open and honest communication. By practicing acceptance and compassion, we encourage others to express themselves authentically and without fear of judgment.

For example, we might refrain from offering unsolicited advice or opinions and instead focus on listening and validating the other person's emotions and experiences.

3. Cultivate Empathy and Understanding: Empathy forms the foundation of deep emotional connections. In this section, we will explore techniques for cultivating empathy and understanding. By putting ourselves in the shoes of others and truly seeking to understand their perspectives, we create bonds of empathy that transcend surface-level interactions.

For instance, we might engage in perspective-taking exercises, imagining ourselves in the other person's situation and striving to grasp their thoughts, feelings, and motivations.

4. Practice Authenticity and Vulnerability: Authenticity and vulnerability are essential ingredients for building emotional connections. In this section, we will delve into the power of authenticity and vulnerability in fostering deep and meaningful relationships. By being genuine and transparent about our own emotions and experiences, we invite others to do the same, forging bonds built on trust and authenticity.

For example, we might share our own challenges, fears, and joys, creating an atmosphere of openness and trust that encourages others to reciprocate.

5. Nurture Emotional Intimacy: Emotional connections thrive on emotional intimacy, a sense of closeness and shared experiences. In this section, we will explore ways to nurture emotional intimacy in our relationships. By creating opportunities for meaningful conversations, vulnerability, and shared experiences, we deepen our emotional connections with others.

For instance, we might engage in deep, heartfelt conversations where we share our dreams, fears, and aspirations, fostering a sense of intimacy and connection.

6. Cultivate Empathy in Action: Emotional connections come alive when translated into actions that demonstrate care and support. In this section, we will explore how to channel our empathy into acts of kindness and love. By actively showing up for others, offering support, and being there in times of need, we strengthen the bonds of emotional connection.

For example, we might offer a shoulder to lean on, provide words of encouragement, or offer help when someone is going through a challenging time.

Technique 36 - Mindful Communication

Dear mindful communicators and seekers of genuine connection, welcome to Technique 36 - Mindful Communication. In this chapter, we embark on a transformative journey of exploring the power of mindfulness in our communication, paving the way for more meaningful and harmonious interactions with others.

Mindful communication involves being fully present and aware in our conversations, speaking and listening with intention, and fostering deep understanding. Technique 36 invites us to cultivate the art of mindful communication, allowing us to communicate with clarity, empathy, and authenticity.

In this chapter, we will explore how to infuse mindfulness into our communication and:

1. Cultivate Presence: Mindful communication begins with cultivating presence. In this section, we will learn techniques to bring ourselves fully into the present moment during conversations. By letting go of distractions and preoccupations, we create space to listen and respond with clarity and empathy.

For instance, we might practice deep breathing or grounding exercises before engaging in a conversation, allowing us to anchor ourselves in the present moment.

2. Listen with Intention: Mindful communication involves listening with intention, truly hearing what others are saying without judgment or interruption. In this section, we will explore techniques for active and empathic listening, allowing us to understand others deeply and respond in a way that honors their experiences.

For example, we might practice reflective listening, summarizing what the other person has shared to ensure that we have understood their message accurately.

3. Speak with Clarity and Kindness: Mindful communication also encompasses speaking with clarity and kindness. In this section, we will learn how to choose our words mindfully, ensuring they are clear, respectful, and compassionate. By expressing ourselves with clarity and kindness, we foster an atmosphere of trust and understanding.

For instance, we might use "I" statements to express our thoughts and feelings, taking responsibility for our own experiences without blaming or criticizing others.

4. Practice Nonviolent Communication: Nonviolent Communication (NVC) is a powerful tool for mindful communication. In this section, we will explore the principles of NVC, which involve expressing ourselves authentically while also empathizing with the needs and feelings of others. By using NVC techniques, we foster empathy and create solutions that honor the needs of all parties involved.

For example, we might use the four-step NVC process of observation, feelings, needs, and requests to express ourselves clearly and compassionately.

5. Embrace Silence and Pauses: Mindful communication understands the importance of silence and pauses. In this section, we will explore the power of intentional silences, allowing space for reflection, deeper understanding, and connection to emerge. By embracing silence and pauses, we cultivate a more profound level of communication beyond words.

For instance, we might practice comfortable silences, allowing the other person to process their thoughts and feelings without feeling rushed or pressured.

6. Navigate Difficult Conversations: Mindful communication equips us with the skills to navigate difficult conversations with grace

and compassion. In this section, we will learn techniques for approaching challenging topics, managing emotions, and finding common ground. By fostering understanding and seeking solutions, we transform potentially divisive conversations into opportunities for growth and connection.

For example, we might use "I" statements to express our concerns and invite the other person to share their perspective, creating a space for dialogue and mutual understanding.

Dear mindful communicators, as we embrace the power of mindful communication, let us strive to create a world where conversations are filled with compassion, understanding, and connection. Through mindful communication, we build bridges of understanding, foster harmonious relationships, and create a space where each voice is heard and valued.

Technique 37 - Reading Cultural Cues

Welcome, fellow cultural explorers, to Technique 37 - Reading Cultural Cues. In this chapter, we embark on a fascinating journey of understanding the nuances of cultural communication, expanding our awareness and sensitivity to the diverse cultural cues that shape our interactions.

Culture plays a significant role in shaping our behaviors, beliefs, and communication styles. Technique 37 invites us to explore the rich tapestry of cultural cues and develop the ability to read and interpret them accurately. By doing so, we foster deeper connections, bridge cultural gaps, and navigate diverse social contexts with grace and respect.

In this chapter, we will delve into the art of reading cultural cues and:

1. Recognize Nonverbal Gestures: Nonverbal gestures vary across cultures and can convey a wealth of information. In this section, we will explore the importance of nonverbal communication, including body language, hand gestures, facial expressions, and eye contact. By learning to recognize and interpret these cues, we enhance our cross-cultural understanding and avoid misinterpretations.

For instance, a seemingly harmless hand gesture may hold a different meaning in another culture, and being aware of such variations helps us navigate cultural boundaries.

2. Interpret Proxemics and Personal Space: Proxemics, the study of personal space and spatial relationships, varies across cultures. In this section, we will delve into the different concepts of personal space and learn how cultural norms influence our physical proximity during

interactions. By understanding and respecting these norms, we demonstrate cultural sensitivity and avoid discomfort or offense.

For example, some cultures have a preference for closer physical proximity during conversations, while others value more personal space. Being mindful of these differences fosters mutual respect and understanding.

3. Understand Vocal Tone and Volume: Vocal tone and volume convey subtle cultural cues, reflecting attitudes, emotions, and social hierarchies. In this section, we will explore how vocal intonation, pitch, and volume vary across cultures and impact communication dynamics. By attuning our ears to these nuances, we deepen our cross-cultural understanding and adapt our communication style accordingly.

For instance, some cultures may value softer-spoken and more melodic tones, while others may prioritize assertiveness and directness. Adapting our vocal style fosters effective communication and cultivates cultural harmony.

4. Interpret Use of Silence: Silence holds different meanings in various cultures and contexts. In this section, we will unravel the cultural significance of silence and its role in communication. By deciphering when silence is used to convey respect, reflection, disagreement, or agreement, we avoid misinterpretations and foster cultural sensitivity.

For example, in some cultures, silence is valued as a sign of respect, allowing others time to gather their thoughts. In contrast, in other cultures, silence may signify discomfort or disagreement. Sensitivity to these cultural cues helps us navigate conversations gracefully.

5. Decode Verbal Communication Styles: Verbal communication styles vary significantly across cultures, influenced by factors such as directness, indirectness, hierarchy, and context. In this section, we will explore the different approaches to verbal communication and the cultural nuances they embody. By decoding these cues, we enhance our intercultural communication skills and build stronger connections.

For example, some cultures value direct and explicit communication, while others prioritize subtlety and indirectness. Understanding these differences allows us to adapt our communication style accordingly.

6. Appreciate Cultural Etiquette: Cultural etiquette encompasses a range of behaviors and customs that reflect respect and social norms within a specific culture. In this section, we will explore the importance of cultural etiquette, including greetings, introductions, gift-giving, and dining etiquette. By familiarizing ourselves with these practices, we show genuine respect for other cultures and avoid unintentional faux pas.

For example, understanding the appropriate way to greet someone or present a gift in a particular culture demonstrates our willingness to honor and appreciate their customs.

Dear cultural explorers, as we delve into the art of reading cultural cues, let us celebrate the richness of diversity and cultivate a deep appreciation for the myriad ways people communicate and connect across cultures. By embracing cultural sensitivity, we bridge gaps, build bridges, and foster harmonious relationships that transcend borders.

Technique 38 - Detecting Emotional Suppression

Welcome, fellow emotional detectives, to Technique 38 - Detecting Emotional Suppression. In this chapter, we embark on a journey of uncovering the subtle signs and signals that indicate when someone is suppressing their emotions. By honing our skills in detecting emotional suppression, we gain valuable insights into the inner world of others and cultivate deeper connections based on authenticity and empathy.

Emotions are a fundamental aspect of our human experience, serving as a compass that guides our thoughts, actions, and relationships. However, in certain situations, individuals may find themselves suppressing their emotions, consciously or unconsciously. This suppression can occur due to societal norms, personal conditioning, or the desire to maintain a composed and controlled facade.

In this chapter, we will explore the art of detecting emotional suppression and:

1. Understanding Emotional Suppression: We will begin by examining the concept of emotional suppression and its impact on individuals. By understanding the reasons behind emotional suppression and its potential consequences, we can approach this topic with empathy and compassion.

2. Reading Facial Expressions: Our faces hold a wealth of information, often revealing emotions that individuals attempt to conceal. In this section, we will delve into the subtle facial cues that can give away signs of suppressed emotions. By observing microexpressions,

eye movements, and facial tension, we can uncover the hidden emotions beneath the surface.

For example, a forced smile or tense jawline may indicate someone's attempt to suppress feelings of sadness or anger.

3. Listening to Verbal Cues: Verbal communication provides valuable clues when it comes to detecting emotional suppression. In this section, we will explore the nuances of tone, word choice, and hesitation that can indicate unexpressed emotions. By attentively listening to the words spoken and unsaid, we can gain insight into the emotional landscape of others.

For instance, a sudden change in vocal tone or the use of vague language may hint at underlying emotions being suppressed.

4. Observing Body Language: Our bodies often reveal what our words do not. In this section, we will delve into the subtle shifts in body language that can betray suppressed emotions. By paying attention to posture, gestures, and physical tension, we can decipher the unspoken emotions lurking beneath the surface.

For example, crossed arms, fidgeting, or avoiding eye contact may indicate someone's attempt to hide their true emotional state.

5. Detecting Incongruence: Emotional suppression can create a disconnect between what is felt internally and what is displayed externally. In this section, we will explore the concept of incongruence and how it manifests in speech, body language, and overall behavior. By detecting these inconsistencies, we can navigate conversations with empathy and curiosity, allowing space for the suppressed emotions to surface.

For instance, if someone shares a story with a cheerful tone but their body language suggests discomfort or sadness, there may be emotions they are suppressing.

6. Creating a Safe Space for Expression: Lastly, we will discuss the importance of creating a safe and non-judgmental environment that encourages emotional expression. By fostering trust, active listening,

and empathy, we can support others in opening up and releasing their suppressed emotions. This chapter will provide practical strategies for cultivating such spaces of emotional safety.

As we embark on this chapter, let us approach the topic of emotional suppression with sensitivity and understanding. By honing our skills in detecting emotional suppression, we can deepen our connections, foster emotional well-being, and cultivate a culture of authentic expression and support.

Technique 39 - Analyzing Decision-Making Processes

Welcome, fellow analysts of the human mind, to Technique 39 - Analyzing Decision-Making Processes. In this chapter, we embark on a journey of understanding the intricate web of factors that influence our decision-making. By honing our skills in analyzing decision-making processes, we gain valuable insights into the underlying motivations, biases, and patterns that shape our choices.

Every day, we make countless decisions that shape the course of our lives. From simple choices like what to eat for breakfast to complex decisions that impact our careers and relationships, our decision-making processes play a crucial role in shaping our realities. However, many factors can cloud our judgment and lead us astray from making choices aligned with our true desires and values.

In this chapter, we will explore the art of analyzing decision-making processes and:

1. Understanding Decision-Making: We will begin by exploring the psychology behind decision-making. By understanding the cognitive and emotional processes that underpin our choices, we can gain a deeper appreciation for the complexity of decision-making.

2. Identifying Motivations and Values: Our decisions are often driven by our underlying motivations and core values. In this section, we will delve into the importance of self-reflection and introspection to uncover the values and desires that influence our decision-making. By aligning our choices with our authentic selves, we can make decisions that bring us closer to a life of purpose and fulfillment.

For example, a person may choose a career path that aligns with their passion for creativity and innovation, rather than solely focusing on external expectations or financial gain.

3. Analyzing Cognitive Biases: Our minds are susceptible to various cognitive biases that can lead us to make irrational or suboptimal decisions. In this section, we will explore common cognitive biases such as confirmation bias, availability bias, and anchoring bias. By becoming aware of these biases, we can mitigate their influence and make more informed decisions.

For instance, confirmation bias may lead us to seek information that confirms our pre-existing beliefs, while availability bias may make us overestimate the likelihood of events based on vivid or recent examples.

4. Assessing Risk and Uncertainty: Decision-making often involves navigating through uncertainty and assessing potential risks. In this section, we will explore strategies for evaluating risks, weighing probabilities, and managing uncertainty. By developing a balanced approach to risk, we can make decisions that strike a harmonious balance between caution and boldness.

For example, in making a career change, understanding the potential risks and rewards, conducting thorough research, and considering fallback options can help us navigate uncertainty with more confidence.

5. Evaluating Long-Term Consequences: Many decisions have long-term implications that extend beyond immediate gratification. In this section, we will delve into the importance of considering long-term consequences when making decisions. By adopting a holistic perspective and considering the ripple effects of our choices, we can make decisions that align with our long-term goals and values.

For instance, choosing a sustainable lifestyle that aligns with our environmental values may require sacrificing short-term convenience or indulgence.

6. Harnessing Intuition and Gut Feelings: Decision-making is not solely a rational process. Our intuition and gut feelings can provide valuable insights that go beyond logical analysis. In this section, we will explore the power of intuition and techniques for tapping into our inner wisdom. By cultivating our intuition and learning to trust our gut, we can make decisions that resonate with our deepest selves.

For example, a person may choose to follow their intuition when selecting a life partner, sensing a deep connection beyond what can be explained by rational analysis alone.

As we immerse ourselves in this chapter, let us approach the analysis of decision-making processes with curiosity and self-awareness. By honing our skills in understanding the complexities of decision-making, we can navigate life's choices with greater clarity and intention.

Technique 40 - Empowering Others through Mindful Feedback

Congratulations, fellow mind readers, on reaching the final chapter of our transformative journey together. In Technique 40 - Empowering Others through Mindful Feedback, we shift our focus from understanding and decoding the thoughts and motivations of others to utilizing our insights to uplift and empower those around us.

Feedback is a powerful tool that can propel personal growth, deepen relationships, and foster a culture of continuous improvement. However, not all feedback is created equal. Mindful and constructive feedback has the potential to inspire positive change, nurture self-awareness, and ignite the spark of personal transformation.

In this chapter, we will explore the art of empowering others through mindful feedback and:

1. The Power of Mindful Feedback: We begin by exploring the transformative potential of mindful feedback. By approaching feedback with compassion, empathy, and a genuine desire to support others' growth, we can create a safe and nurturing space for honest and meaningful conversations.

2. Cultivating Active Listening: Active listening is the foundation of effective feedback. We will delve into the importance of listening with presence, suspending judgment, and offering undivided attention to truly understand the perspectives and experiences of others. By practicing active listening, we create an environment where trust can flourish, paving the way for impactful feedback.

3. Constructive Feedback Techniques: Providing constructive feedback is an art that requires finesse and tact. We will explore various

techniques for delivering feedback in a way that is non-threatening, specific, and actionable. By focusing on behavior rather than personality and offering suggestions for improvement, we can empower others to make positive changes.

For example, instead of saying, "You're always late," we can reframe it as, "I noticed that you arrived 10 minutes later than the scheduled time for our meeting today. Punctuality is crucial for effective teamwork, so I encourage you to strive for timeliness."

4. Appreciative Feedback: While constructive feedback is essential for growth, appreciation and acknowledgment are equally vital. We will delve into the power of appreciative feedback, highlighting the positive qualities, strengths, and achievements of others. By recognizing and celebrating their efforts, we cultivate a culture of encouragement and motivation.

5. Feedback as a Growth Catalyst: Feedback can be a catalyst for personal and professional growth. We will explore how to inspire self-reflection, encourage learning, and support others in setting and achieving meaningful goals. By providing feedback that focuses on development and improvement rather than criticism, we create an environment that fosters continuous growth and learning.

6. Emotional Intelligence in Feedback: Emotional intelligence plays a crucial role in delivering and receiving feedback effectively. We will explore how to navigate emotions and manage potential resistance or defensiveness. By approaching feedback with empathy, compassion, and a genuine desire to help others succeed, we can foster a supportive and growth-oriented atmosphere.

7. Cultivating a Feedback Culture: Creating a feedback culture goes beyond individual interactions. We will explore strategies for fostering an environment where feedback is welcomed, encouraged, and integrated into the fabric of daily interactions. By promoting open communication, trust, and psychological safety, we empower everyone to give and receive feedback with grace and humility.

As we embark on the final leg of our journey, let us remember that empowering others through mindful feedback is not merely about pointing out flaws or shortcomings. It is about nurturing growth, igniting potential, and supporting one another on the path of personal and collective transformation.

In the concluding section of this book, we will reflect on our journey together, celebrating the invaluable insights gained and the profound impact we can have on the lives of others as compassionate and skilled mind readers.

Conclusion: Embracing the Art of Mind Reading

Congratulations, dear readers, on completing this transformative journey into the art of mind reading. Throughout this book, we have explored 40 powerful techniques that have equipped us with the ability to unveil thoughts, motivations, and emotions hidden beneath the surface. We have gained a deeper understanding of human behavior, honed our empathic skills, and embraced the power to connect with others on a profound level.

As we conclude our exploration, it is essential to reflect on the profound impact that mind reading can have on our lives and the lives of those around us. We now possess a unique set of tools and insights that allow us to navigate relationships, communication, and personal growth with newfound clarity and depth.

Mind reading, when practiced with integrity, compassion, and respect, becomes a catalyst for transformation. It enables us to transcend the limitations of surface-level interactions and venture into the realm of profound understanding. By delving beneath the words and actions of others, we unlock a treasure trove of insight, empathy, and connection.

Remember, dear readers, that the power of mind reading comes with great responsibility. As we delve into the inner worlds of others, it is crucial to approach this ability with humility, empathy, and a genuine desire to uplift and empower. Mind reading is not a tool for manipulation or exploitation but a gift that allows us to foster deeper connections and contribute positively to the lives of those around us.

In our journey together, we have explored techniques such as the power of observation, reading facial expressions, decoding body language, analyzing voice and tone, developing empathy, and much more. Each technique has offered us a unique window into the intricacies of human behavior, enabling us to understand the unspoken language that shapes our interactions.

However, let us not forget that mind reading is not an exact science. It is an art that requires practice, patience, and continuous learning. The complexities of human nature can never be fully captured by a set of techniques alone. True mastery lies in the amalgamation of technique, intuition, and genuine connection with others.

As we move forward, let us remember that mind reading is not about using our newfound insights to exploit or manipulate others. It is about fostering deeper understanding, compassion, and growth within ourselves and those we encounter. Let us use this knowledge to build bridges of connection, to heal wounds, and to bring about positive change in our relationships, communities, and the world at large.

With the power of mind reading comes a responsibility to use it ethically and responsibly. Let us honor the trust that others place in us by exercising discretion, respect, and compassion in our interactions. By doing so, we create a safe and nurturing space where individuals can feel seen, heard, and understood.

Dear readers, as we conclude this transformative journey, I invite you to embrace the art of mind reading as a lifelong practice. Continue to explore and deepen your understanding of human behavior, emotions, and motivations. Cultivate empathy, curiosity, and open-mindedness in all your interactions. And most importantly, let the insights gained from mind reading be a force for positive change in your life and the lives of others.

I extend my deepest gratitude to you, the readers, for embarking on this journey with me. May the wisdom and understanding gained from this exploration empower you to forge deeper connections, inspire personal growth, and contribute to a more compassionate and empathic world.

Remember, dear readers, the true beauty of mind reading lies not in its ability to decipher the thoughts of others, but in its capacity to foster connection, understanding, and love in the tapestry of our human existence. Embrace this gift, nurture it with intention, and let it be a guiding light in your journey toward a more empathic and harmonious world.

With heartfelt gratitude and profound

Rami Georgiev

Additional Resources and Recommended Books

Congratulations on completing your journey into the art of mind reading! As you continue to expand your knowledge and deepen your understanding of human behavior and communication, here are some additional resources and books that can further enrich your exploration:

1. "Influence: The Psychology of Persuasion" by Robert Cialdini: This book delves into the principles of influence and persuasion, helping you understand the psychological triggers that drive human behavior.
2. "The Definitive Book of Body Language" by Allan Pease and Barbara Pease: Explore the fascinating world of nonverbal communication through this comprehensive guide, which unravels the secrets hidden within body language.
3. "Emotional Intelligence: Why It Can Matter More Than IQ" by Daniel Goleman: Dive into the concept of emotional intelligence and its impact on personal and professional success, relationships, and overall well-being.
4. "Blink: The Power of Thinking Without Thinking" by Malcolm Gladwell: Discover the power of intuition and rapid cognition as Gladwell explores the world of split-second decision-making and the subconscious mind.
5. "Nonviolent Communication: A Language of Life" by Marshall B. Rosenberg: Learn the art of compassionate communication and how to navigate conflicts, cultivate empathy, and build authentic connections.

6. "The Charisma Myth: How Anyone Can Master the Art and Science of Personal Magnetism" by Olivia Fox Cabane: Explore the traits and techniques that contribute to charismatic presence and effective communication.

7. "The Power of Now: A Guide to Spiritual Enlightenment" by Eckhart Tolle: Shift your focus to the present moment and gain insights into mindfulness, presence, and conscious living.

8. "Crucial Conversations: Tools for Talking When Stakes Are High" by Kerry Patterson, Joseph Grenny, Ron McMillan, and Al Switzler: Enhance your communication skills with practical strategies for engaging in difficult conversations with confidence and empathy.

9. "The Art of Seduction" by Robert Greene: Although primarily focused on romantic seduction, this book explores the intricacies of human psychology and the power of influence in various social dynamics.

10. "Talking to Strangers: What We Should Know About the People We Don't Know" by Malcolm Gladwell: Delve into the complexities of human interactions and the challenges of understanding strangers in this thought-provoking exploration.

Remember, dear readers, that the path of understanding and connection is an ongoing journey. Continuously seek opportunities to expand your knowledge, practice empathy, and refine your communication skills. Embrace the richness of the human experience and let your newfound wisdom be a catalyst for positive change in your own life and the lives of those around you.

May your exploration of mind reading and human behavior be a lifelong pursuit that brings joy, growth, and deeper connections.

Wishing you an inspiring and transformative journey ahead!

About the Author

Hello, I'm Rami, and I'm thrilled to share with you my passion for mindfulness, psychology, and personal growth. With a Master's degree in Psychology and a deep understanding of the human mind, I have dedicated my career to helping individuals cultivate a sense of inner peace, clarity, and fulfillment.

As an advocate for mindful living, I believe that true transformation begins from within. Through my studies and personal experiences, I have witnessed the profound impact that mindfulness can have on our well-being and overall quality of life. It is my mission to empower others to tap into their inner wisdom, break free from self-limiting patterns, and create a more meaningful and authentic existence.

Beyond my academic background, I am also an ardent advocate for conscious living and ethical choices. As a committed vegan, I embrace a lifestyle that promotes compassion, respect for all beings, and sustainable living. I strongly believe that our choices have the power to create a positive impact not only on our own lives but also on the world around us.

Through this book, I aim to provide you with practical tools, insights, and techniques that will guide you on a transformative journey toward a more mindful and stress-free life. I draw upon my knowledge of psychology, mindfulness practices, and personal experiences to offer you a comprehensive roadmap for navigating the challenges of overthinking, finding inner peace, and embracing the present moment.

My hope is that this book serves as a source of inspiration, guidance, and empowerment as you embark on your own path of self-discovery and personal growth. Together, let's unlock the secrets to mindful living and create a life of greater clarity, joy, and fulfillment.

With warmest wishes,

Rami

Don't miss out!

Visit the website below and you can sign up to receive emails whenever Rami Georgiev publishes a new book. There's no charge and no obligation.

https://books2read.com/r/B-A-JXNW-AVDLC

BOOKS 2 READ

Connecting independent readers to independent writers.

www.ingramcontent.com/pod-product-compliance
Lightning Source LLC
LaVergne TN
LVHW090416210926
848480LV00002B/587